to Vickie

PINS & FEATHERS:
THREE PLAYS

b

KATE MILLER, EMMA BLOWERS,
ERIN THOMPSON

PINS & FEATHERS: THREE PLAYS

Coverstory books

First published in paperback & ebook format by Coverstory books, 2020

ISBN (paperback) 978-1-9162899-5-6
ISBN (ebook) 978-1-8382321-0-8

Copyright © Kate Miller, Emma Blowers and Erin Thompson 2020

The right of Kate Miller, Emma Blowers and Erin Thompson to be identified as the authors of this work has been asserted by them in accordance with the Copyright, Designs and Patents Act 1988.

For details on the cover design, please see the Acknowledgements section.

All rights reserved.

No part of this publication may be reproduced, circulated, stored in a system from which it can be retrieved, or transmitted in any form without the prior permission in writing of the publisher.

www.coverstorybooks.com

PINS & FEATHERS: THREE PLAYS

The Last Witch   by Kate Miller

Seeing It Through   by Kate Miller, Emma Blowers and Erin Thompson

The March   by Kate Miller

✤

Kate Miller is a writer, editor and creative writing teacher. Following a career in journalism, she gained an MA in playwriting from Essex University and co-founded Pins & Feathers Productions with Richard Syms. As well as the three plays in this collection, she has written *First Light – a contemporary Passion Play* (2015) and *Plenty of Punch* (2016) for Pins & Feathers. Her other plays include: *The Noose of Light*, about Edward Fitzgerald, the 19th century poet, produced by WriteOn, performed at the ADC Theatre Cambridge; *Circlemakers*, a short radio play, broadcast on BBC Radio Cambridgeshire, produced by Menagerie Theatre, Cambridge; *Another Fine Mess*, produced at the Queen Mother Theatre, Hitchin, Herts; and *Shipton Blank*, one of five winners in Equity / Writers' Guild / Directors' Guild competition, produced at Riverside Studios, London.
www.katemillerwriting.co.uk

Emma Blowers is a local historian and author of: *Around Cold Christmas: A Personal History; Be Ware and Be Prepared: the Boys of St Mary's and the First World War;* and *The Posy Ring: a Victorian Tale of Thundridgebury Manor*. Having had a career in education and with experience in researching the origins of the Scout movement in and around Ware, she became interested in the lives of the young men who served their country, willingly or otherwise, in the Great War.

Erin Thompson writes poetry and short stories, and first worked with Pins & Feathers when she was a volunteer actor in *The Last Witch*. She became involved as one of the writers on *Seeing It Through*, researching the tragedies and comedies of rural village life in the First World War.

✤

Performing Rights – amateur and professional
Applications for performance, including readings and excerpts, for either amateur or professional performances throughout the world should be addressed to Pins & Feathers Productions CIC.

Please email: pinsnfeathers@gmail.com
or use the contact form at: www.pinsandfeathersproductions.com

ⓑ

Contents

Foreword 3

❉

THE LAST WITCH..5

SEEING IT THROUGH 113

THE MARCH..197

❉

Acknowledgements..287

Foreword

Question: why do actors never look out of the window in the morning? Answer: because if they did, they'd have nothing to do in the afternoon.

So it was that, as something to do 'between jobs', the Equity branch in Hertfordshire wrote to writers' groups in the area to see if anyone would like to hear their play read. One Kate Miller from Hertford Writers' Circle offered us the chance to read *The Last Witch*, a play to commemorate the 300th anniversary of the trial of Jane Wenham, the last person in England to be condemned to death for witchcraft. (No spoilers here – you'll have to read the play). An epic piece, with dozens of characters, it was very long. At that first reading in the historic Quaker meeting house in Hertford, after a couple of hours, while the light faded and the pubs beckoned, we hadn't even reached the interval! Discovering issues like that was partly why Kate wanted it read and she used the experience to write another draft.

We were sufficiently excited by the play to think about planning a production, which we did in the studio of Hertford Theatre, with further performances in the village of Walkern, Jane Wenham's home. To cope with its epic quality, we employed a core group of professional actors, and added to them a large number of people from the community, some who had done amateur work, and some who'd never done anything like it before. As well as serving the play well, it was a very rich experience, and many surprising – and lasting – friendships were formed.

At the core of the theatre company we then set up - which we called 'Pins & Feathers' in celebration of witchcraft - we have tried to create intelligent community theatre, often rooted in the history of the places we live, producing new work which connects events to places. We've used local professional actors as and when we could, though Hertford is near enough to London to spread employment opportunities a little further afield.

The plays *Seeing It Through* and *The March* represent another strand of our relating events to places. In both cases, a small group of professional actors took the show to towns, villages, theatres, churches, halls where the material was relevant – in the case of the first, four actors played about 20 parts each! In response to *Seeing It Through*, in several places local people brought their own photos and memorabilia of the First World War to create a small exhibition to go alongside the performance. And in one location, a member of the audience said to one of the actors, "That's my uncle you were talking about".

In bringing these plays together in a book, we hope these dramas, and the true stories behind them, will reach a wider audience. We also hope we might even inspire others to consider a new theatre which, outside the charmed circle of the West End, might relate stories of who we are and who we have been, to and with the communities of which we are a part.

Enjoy!

Richard Syms
Artistic Director, Pins & Feathers Productions

www.pinsandfeathersproductions.com

The Last Witch

By Kate Miller

I first came across Jane Wenham when visiting Hertingfordbury, near my home, where she is buried in the churchyard. Research at the Hertfordshire Archives and Local Studies library opened up the fascinating story.

Jane Wenham was 'The Last Witch' because, on 4 March 1712 at Hertford Assizes, she became the last person in England to be convicted of witchcraft. Her trial was a huge cause célèbre: the comment by the sceptical judge, Sir John Powell, that there was 'no law against flying in England' became famous. The case became embroiled in the politics and religious debates of the day, at a time when Enlightenment thought was making belief in witchcraft seem foolish and outdated.

Despite the many pamphlets published about the case at the time, Jane Wenham's own words are barely documented. Little is known of her beyond that she had lived in the village of Walkern (near Stevenage) for many years, was poor, had been married twice and had one daughter. Almost everything written about her is biased, one way or another: she is portrayed as either an evil witch or a helpless old woman. I wanted to situate her at the centre of her story, but in 1712 her own voice was not heard. Yet she was reported to have had a 'scathing tongue', which was probably one reason she attracted hostility in the first place. In the end I tried to put these contradictions at the heart of the play.

The play, as far as possible, uses what was known about the people involved and shows some of the events which were reported to have taken place. Bizarre and often ridiculous though these were, a woman was on trial for her life because of them.

We were able to stage the play in the places where these events happened: in Hertford and in Walkern, in 2012, the 300th anniversary of the trial.

The 1604 Witchcraft Act was repealed in 1736 (though not in Scotland). Accusations and trials continued after the Wenham case, but no more convictions. Witch hunts persist – the victims and the accusations are ever changing, but the willingness of people to believe baseless allegations, and the readiness of those in power to manipulate popular hysteria, remain the same.

Kate Miller

The Last Witch was first performed at Hertford Theatre on 13 June 2012, with a mixed professional and non-professional cast.

Professional cast

JANE WENHAM	Toni Brooks
ANNE THORNE	Rhiannon Drake
ELIZABETH FIELD	Pamela Kay
DEBORA GARDINER	Lindsay Cooper
REV. GARDINER	Stephen Pallister
JOSEPH ADDISON	Stephen Pallister
MATTHEW FIELD	Lee Ravitz
GEORGE	Lee Ravitz
SIR HENRY CHAUNCY	Peter Mair
ARTHUR CHAUNCY	Ken Boyter
REV. HUTCHINSON	Ken Boyter
REV. FRANCIS BRAGGE	Robert Madeley
SIR JOHN POWELL	Robert Southam
DANIEL DEFOE	Robert Southam
Director	Richard Syms
Musical Director	Christina Raven

THE LAST WITCH

The action takes place 1712 – 1715, in Hertfordshire and London.

Characters

JANE WENHAM	Aged in her 50s
ANNE THORNE	Maidservant to the Gardiners, 17
ELIZABETH FIELD	Walkern village woman, in her 40s
DEBORA GARDINER	Rector's wife, in her 50s
REV. GODFREY GARDINER	Rector of Walkern, 60
MATTHEW FIELD	Elizabeth's husband, stockman to Thomas Chapman
SIR HENRY CHAUNCY	Hertfordshire landowner, JP and antiquarian, 80
ARTHUR CHAUNCY	Sir Henry's youngest son, 28
THOMAS CHAPMAN	Tenant farmer
MARGARET STRETE	Friend of Anne Thorne, 17
THOMAS ADAMS	Landowner and wealthy farmer
MRS MEADOWS	Walkern villager
MRS COOK	Walkern villager
REV. FRANCIS BRAGGE	Sir Henry's grandson, 22
GEORGE	Gaoler at Hertford town gaol
URCHINS	Hertford children
SIR JOHN POWELL	Judge, in his 60s
REV. FRANCIS HUTCHINSON	Clergyman and writer, in his early 30s
JURY FOREMAN	Well-to-do Hertford citizen
EDWARD CURLL	Fleet Street printer
JOSEPH ADDISON	Politician and writer, 40
DANIEL DEFOE	Novelist and journalist, 52
MRS WILLIS	London coffee shop proprietor
DYER	Coffee shop customer
TYPESETTER	Coffee shop customer
TOM and HARRY	London printers' lads
MARY	Hertingfordbury villager, aged 16

ACT 1

SCENE 1

JANE alone on dark stage, in spotlight.

JANE   Our Father...
      Our Father
      Which art in heaven
      Hallowed ... be thy name
      Thy kingdom come
      Thy will be done
      On earth as it is in heaven
      Give us this day our daily bread
      And... give us those who trespass...
      No... Give us this day
      And... lead us not into temptation
      No... Give us
      No...

SCENE 2

January 1712. Walkern. Church End, near to the cottage of JANE WENHAM.

ANNE THORNE is hanging around, apparently waiting. She is 17, pretty, dressed plainly and neatly as befits her position as maid at the Rectory.

JANE WENHAM enters, carrying a sack. She is in her 50s, dirty and unkempt, but vigorous. She hums a little to herself but stops when she sees ANNE.

JANE   You again.

ANNE   What's in the bag?

JANE   Clear off.

JANE sits down, takes some greenery out of the sack and begins to pick through it.

ANNE   Can I help?

JANE   No.

ANNE   You won't let me do nothing.

JANE	Anne – you got floors to scrub at the Rectory, pots to shine, fires to make. Anyway, they'll hurt you.
ANNE	Why? Are they magic?
JANE	No they're nettles.

Pause. ANNE shows no sign of going.

JANE	What do you want Anne?
ANNE	Nothing.
JANE	I know what you want.
ANNE	*(Uneasy)* No you don't.
JANE	I do. It's my job to know.
ANNE	Leave me alone.
JANE	I been watching you.

JANE sorts her nettles.

ANNE	I want… I want you to teach me.
JANE	Teach you what?
ANNE	Everything. I want to be your 'prentice.
JANE	I don't know nothing. Ask anyone. I'm just a beggar and a nuisance.
ANNE	You'll find me a good pupil. I'm quick. Reverend Gardiner has remarked on it. I have learnt to make a hot water crust because Reverend's favourite is a pork pie and I can write my name and count to twenty. *(Pause)* Jane? I can write…
JANE	You're a nincompoop Anne Thorne.
ANNE	You promised you'd teach me.
JANE	I never.

ANNE   When I had that wart. You charmed it off.

JANE   I put a bit of celandine juice on it, that's all.

ANNE   You got the healing touch. I felt it, like a little flash of fire. I could do that, if you teach me. I got powers.

JANE   Fancy. What can you do with these powers?

ANNE   Nothing yet. That's why you must teach me. But I feel a tingle and I know I could do something. Don't you feel like that?

JANE   No.

ANNE   You do. You should be passing your knowledge on, before you die.

JANE   Who's going to die! I ain't that old.

ANNE   You ain't young.

JANE   I'm young enough you cheeky slut.

ANNE   I'm just saying it would be a shame to waste all that craft. *(Giggles.)* Did you know? Mrs Gardiner tries to use herbs. She went down the kitchen garden and got some rosemary and rue for a charm. Didn't work though.

JANE   What was she trying to do?

ANNE   Get rid of spiders from the pantry.

JANE laughs.

ANNE   There's a big one in there, huge. Sits on top of the butter crock. I got a special soup ladle I use for spiders. But every time I whack it with the ladle it comes back to life.

JANE   Really?

ANNE   One day I flattened it. And all this black blood came out of it. I threw it outside. And the next day, it was back! On top of the butter crock, larger than ever.

	And Mrs Gardiner, she can't walk into a room if there's a spider in it.
JANE	So you want to learn a spider charm? Don't you want to make little love charms, sell to your friends? Or were you thinking of something for yourself? Is there something you need Anne?
ANNE	No.

JANE grabs ANNE's face and holds it close.

JANE	What is it Anne Thorne? Why do you want my help?
ANNE	Get off!

Pause.

JANE	When did you last bleed?
ANNE	*(Thinks)* Round about All Hallows.
JANE	Well. It's not too late to do something about it.
ANNE	I didn't say I wanted to do anything about it.
JANE	Then why are you hanging about? *(Pause)* Oh don't be stupid Anne. Just marry that clod of a boy and have done with it. He'll marry you won't he?
ANNE	He'll do whatever I say. I shall lose my place at the Rectory.
JANE	You'll be a wife.

ANNE plays moodily with a stick. JANE sorts nettles.

ANNE	How did you know?
JANE	I can see into your guts.
ANNE	You're a liar Jane Wenham. Do you think Mrs Gardiner knows?

JANE	The Rector's wife knows everything. But not as much as me. What are you going to do with that stick – poke it out?

ANNE throws the stick away in disgust.

JANE	Go away and leave me alone. And don't do anything stupid.

ANNE moves away, sulkily. She bumps into ELIZABETH FIELD.

ANNE	Mrs Field.
ELIZABETH	Shouldn't you be at the Rectory Anne?
ANNE	I'm just going.
ELIZABETH	Were you visiting Mrs Wenham?
ANNE	No.
ELIZABETH	Me neither.

ANNE exits. ELIZABETH goes over to JANE.

ELIZABETH	That girl's Miss High and Mighty since she started work at the Rectory. What's she doing here anyway?
JANE	What are you doing here?

Pause.

ELIZABETH	That stuff you gave me for Ned.
JANE	Didn't work?
ELIZABETH	Jane I think I'm losing him.
JANE	Don't say that.
ELIZABETH	Little lad, he just lies there. It's like he's asleep but not really.
JANE	How many days is it now?

ELIZABETH   Four. When I gave him the herbs like you said I thought they were working. He almost sat up Jane. But then he drifted off again.

JANE   Fever?

ELIZABETH   Same fever.

JANE   Anything else? Spots, colour? Vomiting?

ELIZABETH   Nothing. He's white as a sheet but nothing else.

JANE   Whatever it is it won't show itself.

ELIZABETH starts to cry.

JANE   Come on Elizabeth.

ELIZABETH   I don't sleep myself, I can't eat. I just sit by his bed. I pray of course.

JANE   Of course.

ELIZABETH   I even went to see the preacher at the meeting house.

JANE   What could he do?

ELIZABETH   He's a clever man Jane. He told me to pray. I went to Mr Gardiner.

JANE   He told you to be in church more often I expect.

ELIZABETH   I would. I'd go three times every Sunday if I thought it could save Ned. I'd go for the rest of my life. I thought the Reverend might be kind. He's got children. But he said God gave me the blessing of my boy and if God chooses to take him away from me then I must submit to His will.

JANE   Well bugger that.

JANE goes into her house. She re-emerges carrying a folded leaf.

JANE   Don't touch it until you're ready to give it to the nipper.

ELIZABETH	What is it?
JANE	Nightshade.
ELIZABETH	Just one berry?
JANE	Two would kill him.
ELIZABETH	So poisonous.
JANE	Most things are poisonous Elizabeth, if you have too much.
ELIZABETH	Will it work?
JANE	You know I never make promises.
ELIZABETH	Thank you.
JANE	Don't forget the charm. It won't work without the charm

She gives ELIZABETH a scrap of linen. ELIZABETH tries to make out the words on it.

ELIZABETH	I don't know what it says.
JANE	You don't need to. Sew it inside Ned's shirt. Near to his heart. Better do it when your husband's not around.
ELIZABETH	Matthew won't stop me.
JANE	He'll try.
ELIZABETH	Just because you don't like him.
JANE	I don't know why you married him.
ELIZABETH	You know why I married him.
JANE	Yes well I could have sorted that for you.
ELIZABETH	What do you mean sorted? That's my Suzanne you're talking about.

JANE   I didn't mean it like that.

ELIZABETH   Your tongue can do more hurt than good sometimes. Don't mind about Matthew. He's with some sick cows. *(Hurrying off)* Thank you Jane, thank you.

JANE   Elizabeth – have you…? Anything for me?

ELIZABETH   Oh. Yes. It's not much.

She takes half a loaf of bread out of her apron pocket and gives it to JANE. JANE eats a chunk of it straight away. ELIZABETH exits.

SCENE 3

A few days later. Walkern high road. JANE enters, carrying a bottle of ale.

JANE   A toast. To the cold hearted, muddy faced, empty lardered village of Walkern. Up your arse!

She drinks. ELIZABETH enters.

JANE   Just the woman!

ELIZABETH   *(Seeing the bottle)* Oh Jane.

JANE   It's nothing. Weak as water, the White Lion's brew.

She offers the bottle to ELIZABETH, who declines.

JANE   Go on, drink to Ned. Ned's out of bed, hee hee!

ELIZABETH   *(Taking a sip)* Tastes funny.

JANE   Like someone's pissed in it. *(She takes another swig)* A toast – to my sticks. I found a heap of firewood 'Lizabeth. Not telling you where. Sold sixpence worth this morning. So I'm having a little treat.

ELIZABETH   You shouldn't squander your money Jane.

JANE   Ooh I should save. A penny here, a penny there, soon I'll be rich and a fine lady in furs! No I am one of the lilies of the field, me. Ah talking of fine ladies, 'Lizabeth, here they come.

DEBORA GARDINER, the Rector's wife enters. She is in her 50s, smartly and warmly dressed. She is followed by ANNE THORNE.

ELIZABETH   Good day Mrs Gardiner.

DEBORA   Good day Elizabeth.

DEBORA stares at JANE, who says nothing but takes a swig from the bottle.

ELIZABETH   Good day Anne.

ANNE   It's Miss Thorne. The Rector says in my position I should be addressed respectfully by villagers.

JANE   Of course, in your position…

DEBORA   Anne. What did the Rector say about speaking out of turn?

ANNE   Sorry Mrs Gardiner.

DEBORA   We much enjoyed the curd tarts you made for us at Christmas Elizabeth.

ELIZABETH   Thank you m'am.

DEBORA   You must call in at the Rectory and give Anne your recipe.

ELIZABETH   I haven't got a recipe. But I could tell you how to make them.

DEBORA   I am collecting recipes, to put them in a book. I believe I might get it published in London.

ANNE   'Wholesome country recipes'.

DEBORA   Or 'Recipes from the Rectory kitchen'. That would be very popular.

JANE   Yeh. Everyone knows a parson eats well.

DEBORA   Perhaps '… from a country Rectory'. Curd tarts make a delightful refreshment. Don't you think?

ELIZABETH   Er…

JANE	She don't eat them herself Mrs Gardiner. Do you think Elizabeth's got a larder full of sugar loaf and candied fruits?

Chilly pause.

DEBORA	And how is your son?
ELIZABETH	Much better thank you.
DEBORA	I knew it. My beef tea never fails.
JANE	Beef tea?
ANNE	We cured Ned with beef tea.
DEBORA	With the Lord's mercy and beef tea.
ANNE	It's the first recipe for our book.
JANE	Beef tea cured your Ned?
ELIZABETH	It did perk him up… Matthew said it was very tasty.
DEBORA	Matthew drank it?
ELIZABETH	Ned could only manage a few sips. Would have been a shame to waste it.
DEBORA	It is delicious. Anne has a magical way with herbs.
JANE	What d'you put in it then, Anne?
ANNE	Bayleaf. Bit of sage.
JANE	Bit of onion?
ANNE	Shut up Jane.
JANE	Couple of carrots?
DEBORA	My beef tea could do much to improve the health of this village.

The women speak on top of one another.

JANE I never heard such nonsense.

ANNE Don't you speak to Mrs Gardiner like that…

DEBORA I firmly believe in safeguarding the body as well as the soul…

REVEREND GARDINER and MATTHEW FIELD enter. The women fall silent.

GARDINER Good day ladies. Mrs Field. Jane.

ELIZABETH, ANNE mutter 'Good day sir'.

GARDINER Matthew tells me there is good news about your son, Mrs Field.

ELIZABETH Yes sir.

GARDINER And you have my wife to thank.

ELIZABETH Yes sir.

MATTHEW And the Lord's mercy.

GARDINER Of course.

JANE And some carrots. *(She sniggers)*

GARDINER You are cheerful today Jane.

JANE There's no law against it.

GARDINER Matthew assures me he will be in church on Sunday Debora, to give thanks. This village has a poor record for church attendance in the winter.

JANE Not too good in the summer either.

DEBORA How would you know Jane? We never see you.

JANE I can spy the church porch from my door. I count'em in and out.

MATTHEW People got work to do.

ELIZABETH   And they been going to the meeting house.

GARDINER   Who has?

MATTHEW   It's not against the law now.

GARDINER   Who goes to the meeting house?

ELIZABETH   Oh, you know… People from… Bedford way.

MATTHEW   You're from Bedford way, ain't you Jane?

JANE   No. Walkern born and bred.

GARDINER   Surely not Jane. I remember when you arrived here with your husband. The first one. Which parish were you from? I can't remember.

JANE   Neither can I.

GARDINER   It's a long time since we've seen you in church, Jane.

MATTHEW   You'll never see her. She only goes for her weddings and christenings. And she won't be getting married again. Dried up old hag.

GARDINER   Married again? Surely Mr Wenham is still… with us?

JANE   Somewhere.

MATTHEW   He just won't go within two yards of her.

JANE   Shut up Matthew Field.

MATTHEW   Won't even give you a penny, will he?

JANE   I don't need his money. I got my own.

MATTHEW   From thieving.

JANE   From honest trade. I sold a basket of sticks this morning.

MATTHEW   Where did you trespass to pick those?

22

GARDINER	Oh Jane, not trespassing again I hope.
JANE	I'm not trespassing nowhere! I collected 'em under a tree.
MATTHEW	Whose tree?
JANE	Whose tree? A tree is a tree. It don't belong to no-one except God, eh, Reverend?
GARDINER	Well, er... It depends.
MATTHEW	A tree belongs to a field and a field belongs to a farmer. And if it's Farmer Chapman he won't be pleased.
JANE	Only if you snitch on me and tell him. Here, I got a twig here. Has it got a mark on it, like a sheep? *(She shoves the twig in MATTHEW's face)* Can you see a little C stamped on it?

ANNE sniggers. MATTHEW is furious.

MATTHEW	Chapman won't like it. And you'd better watch out too Anne Thorne. You're always creeping round the hedgerows.
ANNE	I am not.
MATTHEW	I seen you. Collecting stuff.
ANNE	I gather herbs for the kitchen.
GARDINER	I hope not Anne. We have a well stocked garden. There's no need to go grubbing in ditches.
ANNE	Not everything is in the garden.
GARDINER	Surely my wife doesn't send you out into the countryside, do you Debora?
DEBORA	No dear.
MATTHEW	I shouldn't think it's pot herbs, Reverend. More the sort of rubbish Jane collects.

ANNE	That's not true.
MATTHEW	Roots and toadstools.
ANNE	It's a lie. What would I do with toadstools?
MATTHEW	Help Jane make her poisonous muck.
ANNE	I never!
JANE	It's not poisonous!
GARDINER	What is this Anne?
ANNE	I got nothing to do with Jane!
GARDINER	Answer me.
JANE	I don't need that ninny's help. I don't know why she goes out wandering.
GARDINER	You forget yourself Anne. You are an indoors girl now. You are not a field hand any more.
ANNE	I know that!

Silence.

GARDINER	You raised your voice to me Anne.
ANNE	I'm sorry sir.
GARDINER	I had thought you were thankful of a place at the Rectory. Perhaps I was wrong.
ANNE	No sir, you're not wrong. I am grateful sir.
GARDINER	There are other girls in this village who would be eager to have your position Anne.
ANNE	I know sir. I want to keep my position sir.
GARDINER	Then you must show us the gratitude and respect we are due.
ANNE	I am very sorry sir.

GARDINER   Or there will be consequences. Take her home Debora. I shall be back for dinner.

DEBORA   Of course sir. Anne.

DEBORA and ANNE exit.

GARDINER exits in the other direction. ELIZABETH and MATTHEW mutter 'Good day Reverend' as he goes.

JANE   Ha ha. She's in trouble now. Oi, Mr Field. You owe me a shilling.

ELIZABETH   Not now Jane…

MATTHEW   Like hell I do.

JANE   What's a shilling for a remedy that saved your boy?

MATTHEW   A dirty little berry? You think that cured him?

JANE   Yes. Didn't it Elizabeth?

ELIZABETH   I'll see you right Jane.

MATTHEW   You will not. I will not have you wasting my money on her filth.

ELIZABETH   It's my egg money…

MATTHEW   You reckon you cured him. Mrs Gardiner reckons her beef tea cured him. I've no idea what cured him. But I know what ailed him. He was as thin as a stick. I work all the hours of daylight looking after Chapman's cattle and can I afford beef tea?

JANE   Ain't my fault. I saved his life.

MATTHEW   You delude yourself woman.

JANE   Listen Matthew Field. People been coming to me with their troubles for twenty years and they wouldn't keep coming back if my remedies didn't work.

MATTHEW	And I'll tell you something. People get ill. Sometimes they get better, sometimes they die. As far as I can see, no amount of prayers, potions, spells under the pillow, donations to the poor, bloodletting, vomiting or little black berries stops them dying if they're going to die.
JANE	What is it then? God's will?
MATTHEW	God's will is the only thing there is.

Pause.

MATTHEW	There's no cure for any of it Jane. But you women won't let it be.
JANE	Are you going to pay me?
MATTHEW	No.
JANE	Then you can go to hell you miserable skinflint.
MATTHEW	Listen to that tongue. Do you call this woman your friend? She's a nasty witch, like Mr Chapman says.
JANE	Chapman says that?
MATTHEW	He reckons you blighted his harvest last year.
JANE	And does he call me a witch?
MATTHEW	He does.
JANE	May God strike his damned cattle if I don't make him take that back. I won't be called a witch. I shall go to Sir Henry.
ELIZABETH	Don't be rash Jane. It's just words.
JANE	It is not just words! I been slandered, again! Last year Chapman accused me of trespassing, now this. I'm treated with contempt in this village by people who are quick to come skulking round to my door after dark when they have a bad back or their husband can't get it up. I won't be used like this. I shall be heard. I shall have justice.

SCENE 4

Two days later. The drawing room at Ardeley Bury, near Walkern, the house of SIR HENRY CHAUNCY. His youngest son ARTHUR is unmarried and lives with his father. REVEREND GARDINER is with them.

ARTHUR … So we were down to five now because that idiot Feathers got himself unseated in Jenk's Wood and it was obvious she was heading for Benington. And Hemple said, she's got some tricks up her sleeve and this was uphill now, the horses were sweating a bit…

CHAUNCY Arthur…

ARTHUR …But I knew Boxer was up to it, best gelding in Hertfordshire, Hemple's nag was foaming a bit, the hounds were in full flight…

CHAUNCY Arthur one doesn't want…

ARTHUR She was using the hill, see Reverend? To slow us down. Then damn me. I said to Hemple, damn me. What do you think Reverend?

GARDINER Er…

ARTHUR She was doubling back, going downhill. And that was her mistake you see, because half a dozen of the dogs had lost the scent, stupid beasts, when she shoots past them. So that's it, they're right on her tail. She goes to earth but they're on to her, got their snouts right up her hole. When we get there they're like lunatics, scrabbling, whining. Baxter gets his spade – just a few digs, the hounds do the rest. She hasn't moved because she's got six cubs down there. Six! The dogs go wild. You've never seen anything like it. She's fighting like a wolf, blinded one of the bitches, one of the dogs rips her stomach open and she's still fighting, the hounds tugging on her entrails, everyone red and dripping my God it was glorious. Best day this year.

Silence.

CHAUNCY	Arthur has been conducting business for me in London with much success, haven't you Arthur?
ARTHUR	You ride don't you Rector? Come out with us.
GARDINER	It's not for me…
ARTHUR	Nonsense. Make a change from mumbling away in church.
CHAUNCY	If you'll excuse us Arthur. The Reverend and I wish to talk.
ARTHUR	I'm starving anyway. Where's that partridge from breakfast?

He exits.

GARDINER	It is a bad state of affairs, Sir Henry.
CHAUNCY	Hm.
GARDINER	I'm very disappointed. Not so much in Jane – we all know what Jane is like – but Chapman. I thought him a man of sense but…
CHAUNCY	He had a bad harvest. Didn't get enough hands in the field. Wasn't willing to pay. So he blames Mrs Wenham?
GARDINER	Not exactly. I mean, he made no mention of the harvest. He seems to blame her for the deaths of three of his cows.
CHAUNCY	Typical farmer. Cannot accept the vagaries of nature.
GARDINER	I know they will respect your judgment, Sir Henry.

JANE marches in.

JANE	Sir Henry. Reverend. So, have you been talking about me?
GARDINER	Yes, Jane.

JANE	And are you going to tell Chapman he's a liar and a slanderer?
GARDINER	Sir Henry will listen to both sides of your quarrel.
JANE	It's not a quarrel. I got no quarrel with Chapman. I never give him any thought at all. Sir Henry, you're justice of the peace – he's upsetting the peace. I want the protection of the law.
CHAUNCY	He previously accused you of trespassing.
JANE	You can't set foot out of your house without someone accusing you of trespassing.

CHAPMAN and ARTHUR burst in. CHAPMAN has been drinking and ARTHUR has a bottle of port.

ARTHUR	Fought like a wolf! Do you remember?
CHAPMAN	Best ride of the year! Oh look it's the witch.
JANE	You hear him, Sir Henry!
CHAUNCY	Temper your language Chapman. If you have an accusation, make it.
CHAPMAN	She's a thief and a beggar and she's killing my cows!
CHAUNCY	There may be a good reason why your cows are ailing, man.
CHAPMAN	She's got power over animals. She made a pig dance on its head!
ARTHUR	Really?
GARDINER	Oh, that was years ago.
ARTHUR	A pig!
GARDINER	Someone, I can't remember who, swore he caught Jane looking over his pigsty wall and there was his pig, skipping about and, er, standing on its head. He called the neighbours round. Debora went to look. But when they got there the pig had stopped. And they couldn't make Jane do it again.

JANE   'Cos I never done it in the first place.

CHAUNCY   Dance on its head eh?

GARDINER   Debora said it must have been doing something because when she got there it was lying down, puffed out.

JANE   Are you going to tell him to shut his mouth?

CHAPMAN   Are you going to stop persecuting me and my beasts?

JANE   I know nothing about your beasts. You're a mean-minded misery and your brain's shrivelling up!

CHAPMAN   You foul bitch! Sir Henry won't let you talk to me like that.

CHAUNCY   Chapman, what leads you to believe Mrs Wenham has cursed your cattle?

CHAPMAN   I caught her walking near my barns.

JANE   I live near your barns.

CHAPMAN   She looked at me. I knew she meant me ill.

JANE   You told me to go to hell.

GARDINER   Jane!

CHAPMAN   Next day, three of my best cows. Too weak to stand.

JANE   Fool.

CHAPMAN   Witch.

GARDINER   Sir Henry?

CHAUNCY   Godfrey. I cannot see that any causation of material harm has been proven, so it is not a matter for the law. One could say that it is more their souls that are in jeopardy. I leave the decision to you.

GARDINER   Er. Yes. Um. Jane. Treat your betters with respect. If you kept a civil tongue in your head and did an honest day's work you would not find yourself the target of ill-natured rumours. Chapman. These are wild accusations and calculated to provoke unrest in the village. Yes. You shall pay one shilling to Jane as compensation for this slander. Then let that be an end to it.

CHAPMAN   A shilling to that hag?

JANE   A shilling! What's a shilling to him? It's my good name being destroyed.

CHAPMAN   Your good name!

JANE   You insult me, the lot of you. This is calling me a liar to my face when he's the liar. Is this fair, Sir Henry?

CHAUNCY   It is a well meant gesture, Mrs Wenham.

JANE   I got no use for gestures. Well, if I cannot get justice here I shall have it some other way.

She exits.

SCENE 5

A day later. The drawing room at Walkern Rectory. GARDINER is staring out of the window. DEBORA enters, dusting busily.

GARDINER   Debora. What are you doing? Why isn't Anne doing that?

DEBORA   She's hurt her knee. I've told her not to walk on it today.

GARDINER   Oh for heaven's sake.

DEBORA   Said she was looking at a cloud shaped like a haystack, and she tripped over a tree root.

GARDINER   The girl's a ninny! And why is she always out walking when she's supposed to be in here, polishing the silver? I'm beginning to think it was a bad idea, giving her a position in this house. She's more trouble than she's worth. Anne! Anne!

ANNE hobbles in. She is clutching her rolled up apron, which she fiddles with nervously.

ANNE   Sir?

GARDINER   Mrs Gardiner should not be doing the housework while you sit around like some fine lady. Give her the rag Debora.

ANNE takes the cloth. She is feeling faint and is having difficulty standing. She totters and falls.

DEBORA   Anne!

GARDINER   This is ridiculous.

DEBORA   She has fainted. Help me.

They drag ANNE to the middle of the room and try to get her to sit up.

GARDINER   Should we send for the doctor?

ANNE   No! No!

DEBORA   Are you in pain? Lie down.

She takes ANNE's rolled up apron to use as a pillow for ANNE. It feels odd – she unrolls it and a bundle of twigs falls out.

DEBORA   What's this?

ANNE screams.

DEBORA   Anne!

ANNE   No! No!

DEBORA   Is it your knee child?

ANNE   It is no good! I am undone!

DEBORA   See Gardiner? She is in agony.

GARDINER   I can see a lot of nonsense.

32

DEBORA   What hurts Anne?

ANNE   The sticks… I am undone!

GARDINER   What are you doing with a bunch of dirty twigs?

ANNE   Don't touch them!

DEBORA   What's wrong with the twigs? Where did you get them? *(She picks up the bundle and examines them)*. Ow! Anne you stupid girl. Look, she's bound them with a bit of cloth and fastened it with a bent pin. Ow. I'm bleeding.

GARDINER makes ANNE sit on a chair. She slumps, sobbing.

ANNE   I am ruined, I am ruined.

GARDINER   What is this foolery?

ANNE   I couldn't help it. My feet were not my own. She hates this house.

GARDINER   Who does?

ANNE   Jane.

DEBORA   Wenham?

ANNE   She passed by this morning. She has cursed you sir and your house.

GARDINER   Nonsense.

ANNE   Because of the shilling.

GARDINER   She was very rude to me and Sir Henry. But I heard no cursing.

ANNE   I felt it, when she passed in front of the house this morning. I had to get out. The walls were closing in on me. I went out the kitchen door and I started to run. I had to. I ran down the road and I ran and ran. And just by this oak tree there was an old woman. She said stop! And I had to stop…

DEBORA   What woman?

ANNE   …She said why was I going to Benington? I said I was fetching sticks. She said there's no sticks to be had in Benington but she said…

DEBORA   Why were you fetching…?

ANNE   …Lots of sticks in this oak tree. Look it's made of sticks. I said I can't climb it. She said no need. And then the next thing she was at the top of the tree…

GARDINER   That's enough Anne.

ANNE   Right at the top. I saw her. Then she was on the ground again, with a bundle of sticks. And she tied a rag round them and fastened it with a crooked pin. That pin!

DEBORA looks at her finger where the pin pricked it.

ANNE   She said wrap them in your apron. So I did. And then she was gone! And then I came home.

DEBORA   Who was she? Did you recognise her?

ANNE   I couldn't see her face. She had a sort of hood. And since then I can't think straight and I ache all over and my knee hurts…

DEBORA   Gardiner?

GARDINER   I've never heard such a stupid tale.

DEBORA   A tale of bewitchment.

GARDINER   Don't you start Debora! It was bad enough listening to Chapman ranting on.

DEBORA   You cannot ignore this sir. Under your own roof.

GARDINER   If Anne would stay under this roof we wouldn't have so much upset!

ANNE   I ache all over. The house aches all over.

GARDINER   Not another word Anne. Give me the sticks.

DEBORA   Burn the witch!

GARDINER   I beg your pardon?

DEBORA   Burn the sticks, and the pins too.

GARDINER   Debora please…

DEBORA   It is very plain Gardiner, even if you do not want to see it, that these sticks are bewitched. They were given to Anne to do her harm. Perhaps to do us all harm. The pin is bewitched too. It is an evil pin. If we throw them on the fire, the charm will be broken.

GARDINER   Where do you get this nonsense from?

DEBORA   Everyone knows these things. The charm will be broken and the maker of the charm will reveal herself.

GARDINER   How?

DEBORA   It doesn't matter how. She will come forth, whether she wants to or not.

They look at the sticks and the pin in GARDINER's hand.

DEBORA   If you do not Godfrey, I will.

He throws them on the fire. ANNE writhes and moans.

JANE enters the room.

JANE   'Scuse me Reverend, Mrs Gardiner. The kitchen door was open, almost. I need to speak to Anne. What's wrong with her? Shut up Anne and listen. Sir Henry's housekeeper says, can your mother come up to do the washing tomorrow at Ardeley Bury? You ask her and I'll take the answer back. Eh? Speak up. *(She looks at them staring at her)*. Well if none of you got nothing to say, I'll come back later.

She exits.

SCENE 6

The next day. Walkern high road. DEBORA enters, leading ANNE by the wrist. Others follow: ANNE's friend MARGARET STRETE, MRS MEADOWS and MRS COOKE. They gather round ANNE, talking and pointing. ARTHUR CHAUNCY follows, smartly dressed.

DEBORA   Don't crowd her. Give her air…

ANNE   I can't…

DEBORA   You can Anne. Be strong. Don't disappoint Mr Chauncy here. Just one moment sir. Are you ready Anne? Tell Mr Chauncy what you did Anne.

ANNE   I ran.

ARTHUR   Speak up. I don't bite.

ANNE   I ran.

DEBORA   Show Mr Chauncy Anne.

MARGARET   Run Anne!

ANNE tries to run but collapses on the ground, clutching her knee.

ANNE   It hurts…

DEBORA   The devil is in her knee.

ANNE staggers to her feet.

ANNE   I ran and ran.

MARGARET   To Benington.

ANNE   I ran to Benington and back.

DEBORA   And she was only gone quarter of an hour.

ANNE   I must run. Must get sticks.

She begins to stumble down the road. The others restrain her.

Mrs COOKE   How can that be Mrs Gardiner?

DEBORA   It's the truth Mrs Cooke.

Mrs MDWS   She must have been running faster than a horse, eh Mr Chauncy?

ARTHUR   Incredible.

ANNE   Sticks. I need lots of sticks. And straw. And there's none to be found. *(She starts to cry)*. Oh there's no sticks to be found at all. I've looked everywhere, everywhere. Nothing but pins.

DEBORA   And she jumped.

ANNE   I did jump.

MARGARET   She jumped a gate.

ARTHUR   Show us Anne.

ANNE makes a dash and leaps an imaginary gate while the others clap and cheer.

ANNE   I jumped a gate! It was like flying!

She leaps more and more gates.

ANNE   I jumped Manor Farm gate… I jumped Finch's End… I jumped Rook's Nest Farm…I jumped Cabbage Green…

ARTHUR   That's the girl!

The others cheer her on loudly with cries of 'jump Anne jump!'.

ANNE   I jumped the river… Over the Beane, over and back…!

She leaps higher and higher. Her cries and the cheering reach a crescendo. She stumbles, totters and collapses into the arms of ARTHUR.

ARTHUR   This girl needs care. Her life is in danger.

DEBORA   She will recover sir. She twisted her knee, that's all.

ARTHUR	It is not her knee we should worry about, it is her soul.
ANNE	*(Murmurs)* Sticks. I must have sticks…
MARGARET	Should we take her home Mrs Gardiner?
ARTHUR	There is evil in your midst.

The villagers agree.

Mrs MDWS	Been with us for years. We've not had a good harvest since *she* came here.
Mrs MDWS	She came here and nobody knows where she came from.
DEBORA	Cottered, wasn't it?
Mrs COOKE	Dane End, she told me.
Mrs MDWS	She came here without a penny and expected to live off us. And we're not a rich village, are we? Not like some. I've got nothing against strangers but not if they're coming here and taking our bread when we haven't enough to go around.
Mrs COOKE	And look what happened to her husband. Poor old Wenham.
DEBORA	Since he's gone we're without a decent blacksmith.
Mrs COOKE	He was a good blacksmith.
Mrs MDWS	When he wasn't drinking.
Mrs COOKE	She drove him to it.
Mrs MDWS	He'd always drank. He only married her because he was drunk.
Mrs COOKE	Well, he's long gone, Wenham.
Mrs MDWS	He's living with a widow in Buntingford.

ANNE moans.

ARTHUR	Calm yourself Anne.
Mrs MDWS	She's been a curse to this village.
Mrs COOKE	She stole three eggs off me.
Mrs MDWS	She made a pig dance on its head.
DEBORA	I saw that with my own eyes!
Mrs MDWS	I went to her with a toothache and she gave me a stone to put in my mouth.
Mrs COOKE	She gave me a charm for my husband's bad back. Said it was from the Bible but it didn't look like God's English.
ANNE	She picks nettles with her bare hands and they don't sting her! In her house there are bottles of poison and when I went there one day she was boiling a pot and she said it was soup and I looked and floating in it there looked like the head... of a baby!

ANNE gags and retches. She struggles to her feet.

ANNE	Must get sticks.

She tries to run again, lurching off down the street, straight into JANE who is coming the other way. ANNE screams. JANE gives her a sharp shake.

JANE	Stop it Anne.

JANE marches up to the others. MARGARET comforts ANNE.

DEBORA	Mr Chauncy is here Jane. To hear of Anne's marvels.
JANE	Don't waste your time sir. She's daft in the head.
ARTHUR	She is a witness to evil.
JANE	I don't know what the Gardiners have been doing to her but she's losing her mind.
DEBORA	You wish to harm Anne in order to harm my husband. You have always hated us and respectable

	people like Mr Chapman. You are using all your powers against Anne because she lies in a protected place, where God resides in the heart of Walkern, our Rectory.
JANE	I don't hate God's kitchen maid here. Why don't you take her home and see to her knee, Mrs Gardiner, if you ever want her to clean a grate again. Chapman? I don't know what's wrong with him. He's gone bitter and rotten inside.
Mrs MDWS	See Mr Chauncy? She has an evil word for everyone.
ARTHUR	She accuses herself with every breath.
Mrs COOKE	You're not a real cunning woman. Not like that fellow in Aston.
Mrs MDWS	He's a seventh son.
Mrs COOKE	You only got one charm. Stomach ache or a lame horse, you give 'em the same.
JANE	You only need one charm! God will know what you want it for.
Mrs MDWS	We're a poor village and we got a poor excuse for a wise woman.
JANE	There's not a person in Walkern can't point to something I haven't cured for 'em.
DEBORA	Only God can truly heal.
ARTHUR	It is pitiful. I don't blame you people, you can't afford the physician, I know. But we have science now. I myself have attended the vivisection of a dog at St Bartholomew's and seen the circulation of the blood.
JANE	Beg pardon Mr Chauncy. Didn't know you were a doctor now.
ARTHUR	It is the duty of a gentleman to keep pace with the discoveries of our age.

JANE	Your father must be pleased you ain't wasting that education of yours.
ARTHUR	The village doesn't need people like you any more Mrs Wenham.
JANE	You all got it in for me, haven't you.
ARTHUR	I know what you are doing Mrs Wenham. I heard what you said to my father, that you would have justice one way or another. And now I see you torturing this innocent girl. I shall report to my father. Let's get this poor girl home Mrs Gardiner.

They crowd round ANNE with cries of 'Come on Anne', 'Sir Henry will see us right', 'Thank you Mr Chauncy'. They all leave together, noisily, staring at JANE.

SCENE 7

A few days later. Evening. The Rectory drawing room. ARTHUR is standing, smoking a long pipe. There is a knock at the door. ANNE enters, carrying a tray with a bottle and a glass. She puts it on a table.

ARTHUR	Thank you Anne. Shut the door.

She does. She hovers hesitantly while ARTHUR pours himself a glass of port. He offers her the glass. She takes a sip.

ARTHUR	How is your knee?
ANNE	Better thank you sir. I am sure the Reverend will not be long sir.
ARTHUR	Stay a moment. I admire you Anne. Not many young women would suffer your ordeal with such fortitude and… poise.
ANNE	You're very kind sir.
ARTHUR	It is true. But you'll need all your fortitude. It may be that the worst is yet to come.
ANNE	Sir?

ARTHUR		If we oppose Wenham, she will undoubtedly fight back with all her tricks.
ANNE		Oh.
ARTHUR		Don't be frightened. You are not unprotected.
ANNE		No, Mrs Gardiner has been working on a counter spell and buried a witch bottle by the front door.
ARTHUR		Good. And I am here too.
ANNE		It is very kind of you to take an interest in me… in this matter sir.
ARTHUR		I always have the affairs of the village at heart. Besides, this is not some trifling incident. Powerful forces are at work here. What we are seeing in Walkern may be of national significance.
ANNE		Do you think so?
ARTHUR		I do. The eyes of the country will be upon us. There have been predictions of an upsurge of witchcraft and this could be the beginning…
ANNE		Ooh.

He offers her the glass of port again and she drinks.

ARTHUR		Do you have dreams Anne? Since this started?
ANNE		In my dreams I'm running, running, up hill, I'm exhausted, I want to stop but she's right behind me and I think if I can get to a place – I don't know where – I will be safe, but I wake up, and I'm out of breath and sometimes my shift is soaked through with sweat.
ARTHUR		Excellent.
ANNE		Is she causing these dreams?
ARTHUR		Who else?

ANNE	And I dreamt… I dreamt… like in the story I was in a barn, filled to the rafters with straw and I had to spin it into gold and I didn't know how and the straw was cutting my fingers, sticking into me like pins.
ARTHUR	What about the pins Anne?
ANNE	Sir?
ARTHUR	The pins, the pins in your clothing. Where do they come from?
ANNE	I can't say sir. They appear…
ARTHUR	From nowhere?
ANNE	One minute they're not there and the next, it's like little daggers sticking into me… oh!

She squeals and writhes.

ARTHUR	Anne?
ANNE	Get it out! Get it out!
ARTHUR	Where?
ANNE	My back!

ARTHUR reaches his hand down the back of her dress.

ARTHUR	My God! Ow!

He draws out a knot of small pins. He nurses a pricked finger.

ANNE	Sir you are hurt.
ARTHUR	*(Excited)* My God, these are evil pins, evil! Right in front of my eyes.
ANNE	Why is she doing this to me? I'm a good girl.
ARTHUR	Of course you are.

He stands behind her and begins to run his hands over her, feeling along her sleeves and down the back of her dress. He leans to kiss her. She giggles, then pulls away.

ANNE   What's that?

ARTHUR   What?

ANNE   There's someone at the door.

ARTHUR   You said they were out.

ANNE   I can hear scratching.

They listen. There is a faint sound of scrabbling claws.

ARTHUR   Rats.

ANNE   We haven't got rats.

ARTHUR   Then the Devil has sent them.

The scratching sound grows louder. ARTHUR swiftly goes to the door and wrenches it open. DEBORA stumbles in.

ARTHUR   Mrs Gardiner.

DEBORA   I… sir… I … fancy you being here…

There is a sudden, screeching yowl which makes them all jump.

DEBORA   Dear God!

ARTHUR   What in hell's name…?

REV GARDINER enters the room.

GARDINER   This is an unexpected visit sir.

ARTHUR   Damn good thing I'm here.

GARDINER   What?

ARTHUR   Did you not hear it?

They listen. ANNE whimpers.

DEBORA   Shut up Anne.

There is a loud, persistent scratching.

GARDINER   What is that?

DEBORA   Dear God!

ARTHUR   It's God we need. Reverend, fetch a Bible.

GARDINER gets the Bible, ARTHUR shuts the door and puts a chair in front of the door, then goes to check the window. There is another harsh yowl. It sounds unearthly.

GARDINER   What's going on?

ARTHUR   We're under attack by the forces of evil.

The scratching noise grows louder.

ANNE   They're trying to get in.

The noise of claws scratching on wood is abnormally loud and seems to come from all corners of the room.

ARTHUR   Have you a crucifix?

GARDINER   Crucifix? Er, that's a little Papist for me.

ARTHUR   We'll put our faith in the Bible then.

They huddle together, all with a hand on the Bible. The screeching and yowling starts up, weird, echoing, filling the room. ANNE puts her hands to her ears. ARTHUR grabs her hand and puts it back on the Bible.

GARDINER   *(Quoting from a psalm)* The Lord is my light and my salvation; whom shall I fear? The Lord is the strength of my life; of whom shall I be afraid?

DEBORA   Well done dear.

They all listen. There is silence.

DEBORA   The word of the Lord has triumphed.

Another unearthly yowl breaks out, louder than before.

ARTHUR   That's it.

He goes to his coat, lying on a chair, and takes out a pistol. The women gasp.

GARDINER   You brought a gun?

ARTHUR   A militia man is never without one.

DEBORA   I didn't know you were in the militia.

ARTHUR   This is not the enemy we are trained to face, but nevertheless.

He goes to the window and lifts up the sash.

ARTHUR   Pray for me.

He climbs out of the window, brandishing the gun.

ANNE   No Arth…sir!

He is gone. GARDINER rushes to the window, shuts it and peers out.

DEBORA   What can you see?

GARDINER   Not a thing.

Another wave of yowling and scratching fills the room, rising to a crescendo, followed by an enormously loud gunshot, then silence. GARDINER rushes back to the window.

After a while, there is a frenzied banging on the door of the room.

ARTHUR   *(outside the door)* Let me in dammit!

They drag the chair away and open the door. ARTHUR strides in, pistol in one hand, the other holding up by the tail a very large, dead, cat.

ARTHUR   We have been delivered.

GARDINER   Whose cat is that?

ARTHUR   Nobody's. It is an imp sent by the witch. It is the Devil in cat form.

DEBORA   The Devil! In this house!

ARTHUR	Not this. This is a mere bundle of fur and bones. The Devil has gone, fled to she who sent him I expect. But he will be back.
DEBORA	Oh…
ARTHUR	But we will turn his works against him. We have all witnessed what took place here tonight. My father cannot ignore it. We have proof!

He holds up the dead cat, triumphantly.

SCENE 8

A couple of days later. A private room in SIR HENRY CHAUNCY's house. JANE is with SIR HENRY and ELIZABETH.

CHAUNCY	There's no haste. Take as long as you like.
ELIZABETH	Yes Sir Henry.
CHAUNCY	Have you any questions?
ELIZABETH	Sir… am I the right person?
CHAUNCY	What do you mean?
ELIZABETH	I am not skilled in this matter Sir Henry.
CHAUNCY	Few of us are. I have taken advice and I am satisfied that you will do a good job. You are an honest person Mrs Field.
ELIZABETH	Thank you sir.
JANE	I got a question Sir Henry.
CHAUNCY	Yes?
JANE	Will this be it? I mean, will this be an end to it? I come here of my own accord because I want to put an end to all the gossip.
CHAUNCY	I know. I… We shall see.

He exits. ELIZABETH goes to the door, checks there is no one outside and shuts it firmly.

JANE   Don't you trust him?

ELIZABETH I don't trust his son.

JANE strips down to her shift, shivering a little.

ELIZABETH Cold? They got a fire in every room, in this house.

JANE   Yes.

ELIZABETH takes each arm and carefully examines it. Then she looks at JANE's neck and back.

JANE   What are you looking for?

ELIZABETH Sir Henry couldn't say. He said I would know if I found something.

JANE   Lumps and bumps.

ELIZABETH We all got those.

JANE   Not much of a sight, is it.

ELIZABETH *(Attempting to laugh)* Oh you got the body of a young girl Jane.

JANE   No-one's seen it much since Wenham left.

ELIZABETH Well I can't say Matthew's that interested in mine. Prefers to spend time with God instead.

JANE   Does he?

ELIZABETH Oh yes. He doesn't sleep much. He gets up in the night and prays.

JANE   What for?

ELIZABETH Chapman's cows, I think. Should I look at your face?

JANE   I suppose so.

ELIZABETH	He fears Chapman's going to send him packing.
JANE	Why?
ELIZABETH	I must look at your chest.
JANE	To see I ain't got three teats. No, just the two eh?
ELIZABETH	Just the two. Because of the cattle dying. Chapman says there won't be enough work for him.
JANE	Chapman's got scores of beasts!
ELIZABETH	He's a strange man. He's convinced he's losing everything.
JANE	I won't take the blame for people going daft in the head.
ELIZABETH	Hitch up your shift Jane. I must do your legs.

ELIZABETH gets down on her knees to examine JANE's feet and legs.

JANE	Don't forget to count my toes.
ELIZABETH	I'm sure there's ten.
JANE	There's nine.
ELIZABETH	Oh. Yes.
JANE	I lost a little one when I was a nipper. Horse stepped on it.
ELIZABETH	Oh.
JANE	A witch mark is something extra, not something less.
ELIZABETH	I'll have to ask Sir Henry.
JANE	It's when you got something you're not supposed to have. Something that the devil can get hold of.
ELIZABETH	And suckle.
JANE	They say.

ELIZABETH   I'll ask Sir Henry.

JANE   I've had a missing toe since I was five years old. It's no secret.

ELIZABETH   You should get dressed now.

JANE does so.

ELIZABETH   Jane…

JANE   I'm not too worried about the toe.

ELIZABETH   Do you remember that nursing child I had?

JANE   Which one?

ELIZABETH   The one that died.

JANE   That was years ago. You had two or three up from London that you were nursing. I remember one of 'em died.

ELIZABETH   Are you sure you didn't kill him?

JANE   What!

ELIZABETH   I think about him. He wasn't sick. You came to see me and you saw the baby. I think you might have shook his rattle.

JANE   And that killed him?

ELIZABETH   We found him dead in his cot Jane. It was terrible.

JANE   Elizabeth, our churchyard's full of little nursing children. They send 'em up from London, feeble things. The parents don't even come for the burial.

ELIZABETH   I've never forgotten that child.

JANE   I suppose it was hard, telling the family.

ELIZABETH   Matthew made me not tell them for a month, so's we wouldn't have to repay the money they'd given us.

JANE   I didn't do anything.

ELIZABETH   You looked at him Jane. I wonder, perhaps you don't know your own power. You saved my Ned. You gave him his life back. Who's to say you can't take life away?

JANE   Are you telling them I bewitched a baby? What about all the other babies in the churchyard? Did I bewitch them?

ELIZABETH   I'm not telling anything. Nobody has asked me.

The door opens. DEBORA enters the room, followed by ANNE and MARGARET STRETE. They are quiet and purposeful.

MARGARET holds JANE by the shoulders. Calmly, ANNE stands in front of JANE, reaches out to JANE's face and then tries to claw her forehead, digging her nails in as far as she can.

JANE cries out in pain. She clouts ANNE and shoves her to the floor.

ANNE   Did I do it?

JANE   Bitch!

ELIZABETH goes to JANE and DEBORA picks up ANNE. They peer at JANE's face.

MARGARET   No, you haven't.

JANE   Madwoman!

DEBORA   Elizabeth – go to the kitchen and fetch a knife.

ELIZABETH   No!

DEBORA   Anne must draw blood. Then she will be free of the spell.

JANE   There ain't no spell.

ELIZABETH   I shall tell Sir Henry.

DEBORA   See sense Elizabeth. Anne must scratch the witch. Then we'll have an end to this.

MARGARET	She can't Mrs Gardiner. Jane's face is too dried up and hard.
DEBORA	*(Staring at JANE).* Yes. No matter. There will be another way.

She leaves, followed by ANNE and MARGARET.

SCENE 9

A few days later. The drawing room at Ardeley Bury. SIR HENRY CHAUNCY and his grandson, REVEREND BRAGGE, are having a glass of sherry.

CHAUNCY	I dare say you miss Cambridge.
BRAGGE	Truth to tell sir, I have ambitions to go to London
CHAUNCY	I've put word out about getting you a deaconship.
BRAGGE	A position as a Royal Chaplain would be my dream.
CHAUNCY	Francis, you will go far.

They laugh. GARDINER enters, not in a laughing mood.

CHAUNCY	Gardiner. Sherry?
GARDINER	Thank you. Francis. I hope you are well?
CHAUNCY	Any more cats sighted?
GARDINER	Three yesterday. I don't know what today's tally is.
CHAUNCY	Cats with human faces Francis. Been seen all around Walkern.
BRAGGE	Have you seen one yourself?
GARDINER	Not as such.

BRAGGE goes to a table where he has paper and pen set out and starts writing.

BRAGGE	Second of February 1712, widespread sightings of cats with human faces… This must be documented. It is part of my plan of campaign.

GARDINER	Surely it is up to Sir Henry to determine any plan…
BRAGGE	Sir Henry is justice of the peace and will view the evidence we put before him. It is my intention to lead the response of the church…
GARDINER	I…
BRAGGE	You are a stalwart shepherd for the flock of Walkern but you are embroiled in this.
GARDINER	Has the Bishop sent you here as my overseer Francis?
BRAGGE	I have not attempted to speak to the Bishop, as yet. Have you?
GARDINER	No.
BRAGGE	Hm.
GARDINER	Perhaps we should.
BRAGGE	He is a busy man.

Pause.

CHAUNCY	So what is your plan of campaign?
BRAGGE	The palisade round this Christian community has been breached.
CHAUNCY	Francis, the evidence so far is slight.
BRAGGE	Spoken like a lawyer sir. But I see this as a churchman. This is not a crime like, say, arson. We may not find the hayrick burnt, the man seen running away. Evidence must be sought in other ways.
CHAUNCY	Maybe, but my concern is whether I can bring a charge under the Witchcraft Act of 1604.
GARDINER	My concern is whether we're making ourselves the fools of a sick girl and a foul-mouthed old woman.

BRAGGE   Firstly, have you carried out an exorcism of the Rectory?

CHAUNCY   Bell, book and candle? This is not the Middle Ages.

BRAGGE   I can perform the ceremony myself. Be good enough to tell Debora to have the house ready for me tomorrow morning. Now, has this woman's cottage been searched? Talismans, effigies, the tools of her trade will give her away.

GARDINER   Really, Francis, I am not going to play the witchfinder general with my parishioners. Those days are long gone and we do not want them back. We are not Puritans. I feel strongly that, given a decent turnout at church, with a good, strong sermon I can clear the air once and for all.

BRAGGE   Why not let me deliver the sermon? I received plaudits for my oratory at Peterhouse…

CHAUNCY   Thank you Francis, but Gardiner does a very satisfactory sermon. Gentlemen, caution is in order. I will not have mob rule in one of my villages. I do not want houses ransacked, Wenham carted off to be swum – there is to be no swimming! It all gets out of hand. Calm and rational thought is what's needed.

GARDINER   Well said Sir Henry.

The door bursts open and in rushes MATTHEW FIELD. He is an outlandish figure – covered in mud and with straw sticking to his face and clothes. He starts babbling as soon as he sees CHAUNCY.

MATTHEW   She made me do it. It is all her doing Sir Henry. Tell her to stop.

CHAUNCY   Good heavens Field, what have you done to yourself?

MATTHEW   It started with my feet. It was like my feet didn't belong to me. She tried to buy a pennorth of straw. I said what you going to do with it? She said nothing, she said, she sells it to a man who takes it to Luton for hats. I said liar. I threw her penny back at her. And she muttered, you know how she mutters. And then I started to run. I couldn't help myself. I ran and I didn't stop at a gate, I leapt the gate – it was like flying. I was heading for Munden Hill, through the pigs' field and I fell and I rolled in the straw but I kept running all the way up the hill and I got to the top and I shouted 'I'm here!' but there was no-one there.

CHAUNCY, speechless, offers him a glass of sherry. MATTHEW brushes it aside.

MATTHEW   What you going to do about it?

Pause.

MATTHEW   Nothing. You ain't going to do nothing.

GARDINER   On the contrary Field, we have just been discussing this very matter.

MATTHEW   You think I'm mad.

BRAGGE   We have been talking about ...

MATTHEW   Talking? Talking? Master whoever you are?

GARDINER   That's enough Field. The Reverend Bragge is Sir Henry's grandson.

CHAUNCY   Go to the kitchen and get yourself cleaned up man.

MATTHEW   Does it offend you, this mud? This is only on the outside. But what about the cleanliness of my soul? Why don't care you about that?

GARDINER   Matthew...

MATTHEW   I do not fear for myself, I am strong. But this is a village of the weak, Walkern. What other village has a church built by the Devil, eh? They tried to build it on the hill and every morning they found the stones had been carried down to the Beane. The Devil was calling them – come down, Walkern, walk down to the river...

GARDINER   Matthew...

MATTHEW …A church should be on a hill, so that it be the light of the world. What kind of parson are you, that ministers in the Devil's church?

GARDINER That church has been a house of God for 600 years. You'd do better if you attended it more frequently.

MATTHEW How can I, when I feel the Devil's clammy presence as I set foot inside?

BRAGGE Calm yourself man.

MATTHEW Calm yourself! I see here the Church of England. It drinks sherry, it discusses. It quakes in its boots at the thought of confronting the Devil. But I know people who are not afraid.

GARDINER Whom have you been talking to Matthew?

MATTHEW I must have been talking to someone! I could not have seen these things for myself.

CHAUNCY Dissenters.

MATTHEW They listen to me. Their preacher has carried out fifty exorcisms. Witches are a plague in this country. But the Church of England will not stand up to evil and the people know that. Your church will wither and decay like so much stubble. The harvest will have been gathered elsewhere.

He leaves.

SCENE 10

The next day, Ardeley Bury. ANNE and ARTHUR enter, bringing JANE. ARTHUR puts a chair in the middle of the room.

ARTHUR Sit down.

JANE It's alright.

ARTHUR Sit.

ARTHUR pushes her on to the chair, takes off his neckerchief and ties her hands behind the chair. She struggles hard.

JANE	Get off! What are you doing!
ANNE	Shut up.
JANE	Get off me. I'll tell Sir Henry.
ANNE	Sir Henry's orders.
JANE	He didn't order you to tie me up.
ANNE	It's for your own good.
JANE	Bitch!
ARTHUR	If you do not confess we shall prove it.
JANE	You can't because I'm not. Untie me. *(Shouts to the door)* Help! Help!

She struggles and tips the chair over. ARTHUR puts her upright, she kicks him hard. He hits her round the head, so violently that she is dazed and stops struggling.

ARTHUR	Prepare her.

ANNE rolls up JANE's sleeves, lifts JANE's skirts to her knees.

ARTHUR	Can you feel the evil Anne?
ANNE	I can. She is scratching, scratching inside my head. Oh, I tingle all over. Oh! Tingle, itch, oh no, she is scratching me all over, pricking me…
ARTHUR	Where?
ANNE	Help me. Oh!

ARTHUR puts his hand down the front of her dress and draws out a bundle of pins. He goes over to JANE, holds out her arm, takes one of the pins and sticks it deep into her flesh. JANE cries out in pain.

ANNE	Is she bleeding? Is she? There. Stick it there.

He sticks in another pin, and another. JANE struggles but he holds her arm firmly.

JANE	Not this. Stop!
ARTHUR	It is the only way.
ANNE	Find the spot where no blood flows.
JANE	Stop, please. Anne.

ARTHUR sticks in more pins.

JANE	Stop. Sir Henry didn't mean this.
ARTHUR	It is a legal process. Anne?

He gives her a pin. She sticks it in JANE's other arm.

ANNE	I shall find the spot where she can't bleed.
JANE	I am bleeding. Stop it.
ARTHUR	You have a witch spot, where no blood flows. It proves who you are, a dried up old hag, the Devil has sucked all the juice out of you.
ANNE	Oh… oh…
ARTHUR	What is it?
ANNE	Help me. She is fighting back. I suffer.

She totters as if to faint and ARTHUR holds her. They kiss passionately. ARTHUR pushes his hands up her skirts and they get increasingly excited. Suddenly he yelps in pain and breaks off kissing. He withdraws his hand, holding another bundle of pins.

ARTHUR	Oh God, Anne! My poor Anne. We shall turn her weapons against her.
JANE	You're mad. Both of you. I'll tell Sir Henry.
ANNE	He won't believe a witch.

They kneel down and start sticking pins into JANE's legs. She howls in pain.

JANE	Stop this. Stop it. You'll be sorry.
ARTHUR	She's threatening us.
ANNE	Look, look, here. No blood. A sort of liquid coming out, clear liquid. Disgusting. Ooh…

JANE is dazed and weak with pain. Blood is streaming down her arms.

ARTHUR and ANNE are in each other's arms.

ANNE	Do you dare?

They kiss passionately.

SCENE 11

The same room. Two days later. JANE is tied to the chair. The blood has been cleaned up. BRAGGE is at a table, pouring a glass of water from a jug.

JANE's head is lolling. She nods forward, about to drop off to sleep. BRAGGE throws the glass of water in her face and she jerks awake. Stares at him.

JANE	Sir?

SIR HENRY CHAUNCY and REV GARDINER enter.

CHAUNCY	Francis. How are we doing?
BRAGGE	Well sir. She has not slept for two days.
CHAUNCY	Untie her.

GARDINER unties her. CHAUNCY goes to the sideboard and pours her a glass of port. She sips it unsteadily.

JANE	So? Am I a witch?
CHAUNCY	You must tell us Jane.
JANE	Mr Chauncy's done his test to find a mark. Am I a witch?
CHAUNCY	It is not a reliable test.

JANE	I know I am not a witch. I want to prove it. Let me swim for it.
GARDINER	Jane, you will drown, to no purpose.
BRAGGE	Water is not a reliable test either.
CHAUNCY	We must keep this civil.
BRAGGE	Mrs Wenham. You must confess.
JANE	I have done nothing. I give you my word.
BRAGGE	We cannot take that. The Devil is the arch-liar. We must make objective tests.
JANE	I shall die of it sirs.
GARDINER	No Jane. We shall not touch you. You know the Lord's Prayer, do you not?
JANE	Of course sir.
GARDINER	Then say it.
JANE	Now?
BRAGGE	All the way through.
JANE	You know I know it Reverend Gardiner.
GARDINER	You must recite it without fault. It is the truest test. If you have a clear conscience you will not stumble.

JANE hesitates.

GARDINER	Go on Jane.
JANE	Our Father…
BRAGGE	Speak up.
JANE	Our Father Which art in heaven Hallowed be thy name…

(Pause)

The words are flying around my head. I do know it sirs.

(She tries again)

Our Father
Which art in Heaven
Hallowed be thy name
Thy kingdom come
Thy will be done
On earth as it is in heaven
Give us this day our daily bread
And forgive us our trespasses…
…As we forgive them that trespass against us.
And lead us not into no temptation…

BRAGGE   What?

JANE   What?

BRAGGE   That wasn't right.

JANE   What wasn't?

GARDINER   Say it again.

JANE   My… I… If I could have some sleep…

GARDINER   You must undergo this test Jane. The Lord's Prayer cannot lie.

JANE   Our Father
Which art in Heaven
Hallowed be thy name
Thy kingdom come
Thy will be done
On earth as it is in heaven
Give us this day our daily bread.
And forgive us our trespasses
As we forgive them that trespass against us.
And lead us into temptation
But deliver us from evil…

BRAGGE   There! Did you hear it?

CHAUNCY	What?
BRAGGE	She said it. The Devil is in her tongue.
CHAUNCY	What did she say?
BRAGGE	Lead us into temptation. She said it. Lead us into temptation.
JANE	I didn't!
GARDINER	I heard it.
JANE	I know the prayer! Let me say it again.
BRAGGE	No need. We have clear proof.
CHAUNCY	Remarkable. Such a simple test.
GARDINER	Humane.
JANE	Let me say it again…
BRAGGE	Infallible. 'Lead us into temptation'. We all heard it.

Pause. JANE sobs quietly.

BRAGGE	You must confess now.
JANE	I've nothing to say sir.
BRAGGE	How long have you been a witch?
JANE	I'm not.
BRAGGE	What are you then? A wise woman? A charmer? What do you call yourself?
JANE	I don't call myself anything.
BRAGGE	But you dispense charms, remedies
JANE	I try to help people.
BRAGGE	How long has she been in Walkern Reverend?

GARDINER	Fifteen, sixteen years.
BRAGGE	Sixteen years a witch!
JANE	No…
BRAGGE	An instrument of the Devil.
JANE	I don't know nothing about the Devil. I have a bit of knowledge and I help people if I feel like it.
BRAGGE	Knowledge? God works through you, does he?
JANE	I don't say that. But I do know things.
BRAGGE	You are in the Devil's snare like Miriam, sister of Moses, when she claimed to be a prophet. And the Lord came down in the pillar of the cloud. And the anger of the Lord was kindled against her. And the cloud departed and behold, Miriam became leprous, white as snow.

Silence.

BRAGGE	Confess Mrs Wenham…
CHAUNCY	Francis. We have enough. I am satisfied.
JANE	Satisfied! Yes, you have satisfaction now. I stumbled in the prayer – ha! You have me. Look at you – three men of God. Three black carrion crows. Three blackened footpads, lurking behind the trees. Lying in wait for my life!
BRAGGE	What about the others sir? She must name others. Witches do not practise alone. It has been proven on good authority.
CHAUNCY	This will do…
BRAGGE	You know other servants of the Devil…
JANE	Do I?
BRAGGE	Who are they? Speak!

JANE   Anne Thorne, Debora Gardiner…

GARDINER   That's enough!

JANE   Debora, Anne…

CHAUNCY goes to the door and opens it.

CHAUNCY   Come! Take her now.

A watch guard enters and seizes JANE.

CHAUNCY   Mrs Wenham you are under arrest on charges of witchcraft. Take her away. Go on, get her out of here!

JANE is bundled out.

End of ACT 1.

ACT 2

SCENE 1

Two weeks later, February 1712. A cell in Hertford town gaol. JANE is in leg irons. GEORGE, the town gaoler, enters. He throws her a chunk of bread.

JANE	I hope this is better than yesterday's filth.
GEORGE	All food comes from the Lord.
JANE	It's disgusting! Covered in mould.
GEORGE	Mould comes from the Lord.
JANE	He can keep it.
GEORGE	Usually, people's friends bring them food.
JANE	And I'm perishing cold.
GEORGE	You got blankets.
JANE	I got one blanket. And that's mostly holes.
GEORGE	Usually, people's friends bring them blankets.
JANE	You should look after me more. Sir Henry won't be pleased if they find me starved and dead in here one morning.
GEORGE	Remember John Owen, the highwayman? He was in here. You should have seen the stuff people brought him. He had jugged hare, he had claret, he had pheasant. I did very well on the leftovers. He had a clean linen shirt every day. His wife brought one one day and his mistress the next. This is one of his shirts I'm wearing now. Look, feel the quality.
JANE	Gave it you as a mark of gratitude did he?
GEORGE	He left it behind. When they hanged him.

Pause.

GEORGE	He had money you see, Owen. Stolen, of course. But money brings you friends.
JANE	Here. I got no money but I got powers. I expect you've heard. I got this charm. It's a very good charm. Bring me a bit of paper and I can write it down for you and you wear it inside your nice linen shirt. It makes a very good love charm.
GEORGE	I'm married.
JANE	And it's a very good charm for finding buried treasure. I bet there's a lot of buried treasure in Hertford. All the kings and queens who stayed here.
GEORGE	Ha!
JANE	Well?
GEORGE	No thanks. Come on.
JANE	What? *(frightened)* Are they coming to get me?
GEORGE	You can go out in the yard.
JANE	Outside? You said I'm not allowed outside.
GEORGE	Get a move on.

With difficulty, JANE shuffles in her chains out of the door and into the yard. At first she shields her eyes from the light. Then she begins to look around her. She shuffles into the middle of the yard and stands there, staring up at the sky.

George roams up and down the yard, impatiently.

GEORGE	Go on then. Walk.
JANE	What, with these on? *(Indicating the leg irons)*
GEORGE	Come on Jane. I'm doing you a favour, getting you some air.

She shuffles and clanks around.

| JANE | Take 'em off George. |

GEORGE	Please.

JANE	Please.

GEORGE	No. I got my orders.

JANE	What are you afraid of?

GEORGE	I'm not afraid of anything. Except what Sir Henry's going to say if I'm caught taking your irons off.

JANE	Afraid I might fly off?

GEORGE laughs.

JANE	Afraid I might fly like a bird to the top of that tree?

GEORGE	You can't fly.

JANE	I'll perch at the top of that tree, looking down at you. I'll look all around and think, where shall I fly to? Perhaps south, to London. Or perhaps I'll go that way and when I pass over Walkern I'll swoop down and shit on everybody. Then I'll fly north and be gone.

GEORGE	You can't fly woman.

JANE	I can. With the Devil's aid.

GEORGE	Jane. I've watched you in that cell for the past five days and the Devil has not come to your aid. He hasn't burst your chains, he hasn't flung open the door, he hasn't even turned you into a rat so you can scuttle out the drain. You haven't got any magical powers.

JANE	So why am I here?

GEORGE	Because you're a rotten old maggot who hasn't enough sense not to go upsetting the gentry.

JANE	Take my irons off then.

GEORGE	I can't.

JANE	You got the key.
GEORGE	I got my orders.

Pause.

JANE	If you don't think I'm a witch, perhaps the jury won't either.
GEORGE	Perhaps.
JANE	Sir Henry knows I'm not a witch.
GEORGE	Really? Why did he put you in here then?

JANE sulkily shuffles forward. She looks up at the tree overhanging the yard.

JANE	It's good to see a tree, all the same. Hey!
GEORGE	What?
JANE	There's someone up there. In the branches. It's a lad. Look – there's more of 'em.
GEORGE	Oi! You!
JANE	Little buggers!
GEORGE	*(Shouting up at the tree)* What did I tell you? Farthing to see the witch. Come on! Pay up!

Coins come flying down into the yard. GEORGE goes round picking them up, then calls up again.

GEORGE	Make room and let the others see!
JANE	What's all this?
GEORGE	Farthing each! You there! Farthing to see the witch.

More coins come raining down. JANE tries to get one, GEORGE pushes her aside. JANE looks up and sees faces in the tree, gawping at her and laughing.

JANE	You grasping devil George.

GEORGE laughs.

68

JANE	I have powers. May these coins choke you! May you wake in the night unable to breathe. May your cock shrivel up like a dried leaf and fall off one morning like a leaf in autumn. See if this doesn't come true.

Pause.

GEORGE	Make your mind up woman. Do you want to be a witch or don't you? Eh? Do you want to hang or not? It's all the same to me. I don't believe in that nonsense. But people think you're a witch. They like thinking you're a witch. I don't know why they do but *(he holds out the coins)* it's all good for me.

SCENE 2

Late February 1712. A comfortable room at The Bell Inn, Hertford. The judge, SIR JOHN POWELL, is reading through a sheaf of papers, chuckling to himself from time to time. SIR HENRY CHAUNCY stands, waiting for him to finish reading.

CHAUNCY	What do you think?
POWELL	Very entertaining.
CHAUNCY	John...
POWELL	I know, it is a serious matter. But I do like the demon cats.
CHAUNCY	People are frightened to leave their homes in case they see one.
POWELL	I don't doubt it.
CHAUNCY	You have experience of similar cases.
POWELL	Yes and similar evidence. Quite recently, down in Somerset. Two women had been turned into stone by their neighbour, they assured me. Fortunately they had recovered movement in their limbs by the time I saw them and seemed no worse for their ordeal.
CHAUNCY	What was the outcome?

POWELL	Not guilty. The case should never have proceeded to court.
CHAUNCY	And what do you think of the quality of our depositions? You agree with me there is a case under the Act?
POWELL	The Witchcraft Act is a hundred and seven years old Sir Henry. It dates from a time when people thought the sun circulated round the earth.
CHAUNCY	Most people still think so.
POWELL	But is it the law's job to perpetuate ignorance?
CHAUNCY	I believe a felony has been committed.
POWELL	I am merely saying, sir, that there has not been a guilty verdict in a witchcraft case for 28 years. You are bringing a charge under a feeble law.
CHAUNCY	You would not get rid of the Act?
POWELL	Sooner or later the modern thinkers will propose it to Parliament.
CHAUNCY	It would be shameful. What sort of Christian nation would we be, if we had no weapons against the Devil in our armoury of statutes?
POWELL	Indeed, but I rarely see these arms being used against the Devil, only by one peevish neighbour against another.

Pause.

POWELL	This Anne Thorne, I take it, is your chief witness?
CHAUNCY	Yes, Anne Thorne. Hm… Her health is not good. But I am sure she will rally to speak in court.
POWELL	Any witnesses in favour of Mrs Wenham?
CHAUNCY	No.
POWELL	She is so unpopular?

CHAUNCY   In the village, yes. To tell the truth, I do not dislike her. But others hear only her scathing tongue.

POWELL   If I may speak candidly…

CHAUNCY   Of course.

POWELL   I do not like the case. I do not see evidence of evil at work. I see some strange events – I grant you – but no-one much hurt. What I do see is bad temper and girlish foolery and peasant superstition that has addled the brains of everyone in the vicinity.

CHAUNCY   I thought so too John, at first. But there is real evil at work.   Look at the victims in this case – the Rector, my own son. These are not common folk. The authority of God and the rule of law are under attack here.

POWELL   I share your concern…

CHAUNCY   Sir, authority is threatened everywhere in England today. Hertford itself is a nest of Quakers. Dissent is preached in every town. The foundation stones of the Church are being chipped away.

POWELL   We are men of the law, not of the church.

CHAUNCY   It is all one. What would our law be if it were not a Christian law? It would be the law of tyrants. You and I, John, we are old enough to remember what tyranny is…

POWELL   Well I was a child when Cromwell died… Let's be truthful – that tyranny was done mostly in the name of God.

CHAUNCY   Indeed, and we are rightly suspicious of the fanatics who claim they have their cause direct from God, which puts them above the law. But we have gone too far the other way. The Church christens people, marries them, buries them. The people don't expect more and the parsons don't give it. But is that enough? The packed dissenters' meeting houses tell me no.

POWELL   Shouldn't we leave this to the divines, Henry? The talk in London is always of the church.

CHAUNCY   Yes, yes. Factions in the church, high, low, Whig, Tory. It is all a struggle for dominance among the parties, not about religion. *(Pause)* I don't claim to know about matters theological. But I cannot stand by and see people near me under attack. The law is nothing if it does not protect the soul as well as the body.

POWELL   You have a jury to convince. The good men of Hertford will not want to look superstitious.

CHAUNCY   This case cannot be set aside, John. The hornet's nest has already been disturbed. Keeping the peace becomes more of a struggle each year. A bad harvest is a disaster. The poor are ever more of a burden.

POWELL   And if Mrs Wenham hangs, will that help the peace?

CHAUNCY   The law must be seen to take its course.

SCENE 3

The next day. Hertford gaol. JANE is still in leg irons. GEORGE enters.

GEORGE   A friend.

He shows in ELIZABETH FIELD, who is carrying a basket. He hangs around.

JANE   You don't have to stay.

GEORGE   I do.

JANE   In case she smashes these irons with an axe and escapes with me on a team of horses.

GEORGE exits.

ELIZABETH   Jane.

JANE   What have you brought me?

ELIZABETH gives her some ham and bread. JANE starts eating immediately.

JANE   Drink?

ELIZABETH hands her a bottle of beer.

ELIZABETH   Who has been to see you?

JANE   Nobody.

ELIZABETH   It is quiet in the village.

JANE   No more cats?

ELIZABETH   The cats are being seen in Hertford. And Ware too.

JANE   Huh.

ELIZABETH   Anne Thorne is poorly. They say she has lost her wits. She may not give evidence at the trial.

JANE pauses.

ELIZABETH   It will make no odds Jane. Everyone knows her story. It is gospel now.

JANE   Ain't you got nothing good to tell me?

ELIZABETH   Two more of Chapman's cows died. *(Pause)* I keep having dreams.

JANE   About me? Am I to hang or not?

ELIZABETH   Not about you. About that baby.

JANE   It had a Christian burial, didn't it?

ELIZABETH   I was walking down the high road. The birds were flying all about, with straw in their beaks to make nests. And I saw the baby, by the side of the road. He opened his mouth and he sang, like a bird. The song went right through my body. Then I woke up. What does it mean? Jane?

GEORGE enters, carrying a chair.

GEORGE   Unbelievable.

JANE   What?

GEORGE   You got a visitor.

He puts the chair down and polishes it with his handkerchief.

JANE   I know.

GEORGE   Not her. A real visitor.

JUSTICE POWELL enters.

GEORGE   Sir.

POWELL   Thank you George.

GEORGE   This is Mrs Wenham sir. This one.

POWELL   So I see.

GEORGE   The other one's just a woman sir.

POWELL   Thank you George.

GEORGE   Shall I stay sir?

POWELL   I shall be quite safe thank you.

GEORGE exits.

POWELL   Mrs Wenham.

He shakes her hand, to her astonishment.

JANE   Sir.

He turns to ELIZABETH and shakes her hand.

POWELL   And Mrs…?

ELIZABETH   Field sir. Elizabeth Field. Of Walkern.

POWELL   You are a friend of Mrs Wenham?

ELIZABETH   Yes sir.

POWELL	I am Mr Justice Powell. I shall be the judge in your trial.
JANE	Sir.
POWELL	I have read the accounts of the witnesses. A farrago of nonsense.
JANE	Ha!
POWELL	In my opinion. However, I warn you it is not my opinion which counts, but that of the jury.
ELIZABETH	But sir – Anne, Reverend Gardiner, Mr Chauncy – we all know what happened to them.
POWELL	We do. But was it Jane that caused it?
JANE	So. Have you come to see for yourself if I am a witch?
POWELL	Mrs Wenham. In my thirty years as a judge I am confident I have never met a witch. I would be surprised to find my first one in Hertford.
JANE	Oh.
POWELL	I wanted to see you. You are a widow?
JANE	Sort of.
POWELL	You live alone, I take it? With little to support you.
JANE	Sir.
POWELL	I have presided over many witchcraft trials Mrs Wenham. And there is nearly always a woman of your type accused…
JANE	My type…
POWELL	… An ordinary village woman, of advancing years, who has the misfortune to find herself the target of the vicious gossip and jealous resentment that festers in a small society.

JANE	Huh.
POWELL	I want the jury to hear these extravagant claims of magical occurrences and demonic possession and for them to look at you, a humble figure, and see that you could not possibly be responsible for them.
JANE	Oh. *(Pause)* Because I'm a nobody.
POWELL	You are Mrs Wenham's friend? I see you have brought her food.
ELIZABETH	Yes sir.
POWELL	Would you like to speak in her defence? It is permitted.
ELIZABETH	Matthew – my husband – wouldn't…
POWELL	You would be serving the law of the land. I would not subject you to harsh questioning. You may say in simple terms that in your experience Mrs Wenham is an ordinary woman, with no supernatural powers.
ELIZABETH	Well, my Ned…
POWELL	I beg your pardon?
ELIZABETH	No-one will be interested in what I have to say, sir. I do not work for a gentleman.
POWELL	But you are a sensible woman, a wife. Will you speak?
ELIZABETH	If you wish it sir.
POWELL	I do. Now, Mrs Wenham, you must be ready to give your own account of the events to the court.
JANE	I have no skill at speech, sir.
POWELL	I do not think that is true.
JANE	I am a humble woman sir. You just said.
POWELL	But you are not a fool.

JANE	No one will hear me. They have made up their minds.
POWELL	In the village. But not in the town. Choose your words and you have every chance of acquittal.

SCENE 4

The same day. Fleet Street, London. EDWARD CURLL, a printer, enters from one side, FRANCIS BRAGGE from the other.

BRAGGE	Excuse me sir, do you know Fleet Street?
CURLL	All too well.
BRAGGE	I'm looking for Mr Curll, the printer. I was directed to some rat-infested yard…
CURLL	Curll? Who wants him?
BRAGGE	Er, I do.
CURLL	Edward Curll at your service Reverend.
BRAGGE	I have some interesting information.
CURLL	About what?
BRAGGE	The Hertfordshire witch.
CURLL	Yeh. Got lots of stuff on that.
BRAGGE	By whom?
CURLL	I'm not at liberty to reveal my sources.
BRAGGE	I do not think they can have as intimate knowledge of the events as I. *(Pause)* I am Francis Bragge.
CURLL	Oh yeh?
BRAGGE	Grandson of Sir Henry Chauncy. The well known author and prosecutor of the celebrated witchcraft case?

CURLL   Go on.

BRAGGE   I personally led the testing of the witch. I have witnessed her crimes at first hand.

CURLL   And you've written something for publication?

BRAGGE shoves a sheaf of papers into CURLL's hand. CURLL looks at them.

CURLL   Do you want this anonymous?

BRAGGE   I suppose so.

CURLL leafs through the papers.

BRAGGE   How much?

CURLL   Twenty.

BRAGGE   Fifty.

CURLL   Thirty.

They shake hands.

SCENE 5

The court house, Hertford, 4 March 1712. POWELL is in a private room, preparing to go into court. REV FRANCIS HUTCHINSON enters.

HUTCHS'N   My lord…

POWELL   What sort of turn-out have we got?

HUTCHS'N   My lord, the courtroom is packed. As was the coach up from London.

POWELL   The innkeepers are rejoicing.

HUTCHS'N   This is a most significant case my lord. A great responsibility lies on your shoulders.

POWELL   And you are?

HUTCHS'N   I beg your pardon. Reverend Francis Hutchinson, of Suffolk. I have a profound interest in these matters.

POWELL   I'm afraid Reverend, if you think this case will give you firm evidence of the Devil at work in the land, you will be disappointed.

HUTCHS'N   No no my lord. It is an embarrassment to me to see men of my own church beguiled by this witchcraft nonsense. I say so in my book.

POWELL   You have written a book?

HUTCHS'N   Er… I have not published it yet, but I feel I must speak out if the Church of England is not to slide into superstition. I mean, my lord, do you not find witchcraft trials offensive to the disciplines of the law? The ridiculous evidence that is permitted. In other cases, a person charged can clear himself by showing he was, for example, at home when the crime was committed. But in prosecutions for witchcraft, if some crack-brained girl claims an old woman is pursuing her in visions, the witchcraft believers cry 'compact with the devil' and hang the accused for things that they were supposedly doing, when they were asleep in bed, or even in gaol with double irons on them!

POWELL laughs and slaps him on the back.

POWELL   My boy – you are an ornament to the Church and a loss to the legal profession! Do not fear – the outcome of this trial will give no encouragement to the witchcraft believers. But I must go through now.

He moves to the courtroom, which is packed. JANE is in the dock, manacled. The 12 jurymen are in place. Among the witnesses, ANNE is there with DEBORA, REV GARDINER, ARTHUR CHAUNCY, FRANCIS BRAGGE, MARGARET STRETE, FARMER CHAPMAN, THOMAS ADAMS and ELIZABETH.

The hubbub of voices rises and then dies down as POWELL takes his seat. He looks out over the crowd of observers and witnesses.

POWELL   What a lot of women. Perhaps we should look for witches not among the old women but among the young ones. Wouldn't that be more amusing?

There is laughter at this. POWELL looks pleased.

ANNE	What does he mean?
DEBORA	You're the one performing wonders Anne.
ANNE	I'm the victim!
POWELL	Gentlemen of the petty jury. The evidence having been presented to the grand jury and the bill found to be true, the defendant, Jane Wenham of Walkern in the county of Hertfordshire stands before you at these assizes indicted for conversing familiarly with the Devil in the shape of a cat.
BRAGGE	What about Anne?
POWELL	That is the indictment.
BRAGGE	She should be standing trial for the suffering inflicted on this poor innocent girl.
POWELL	The law demands evidence of a diabolic pact. In this case it appears it is all to do with cats.
BRAGGE	Disgraceful.
POWELL	Gentlemen of Hertford. You will hear numerous items of evidence presented by the denizens of this minor village. I beg you to listen attentively and make up your own minds. Mrs Gardiner.

DEBORA comes forward.

POWELL	You were present when these events began.
DEBORA	I was sir.
POWELL	Please relate.
DEBORA	Well, Mr Chapman had been saying for some months that he was losing cattle and couldn't tell why…
POWELL	Mrs Gardiner. The events as witnessed by you.

DEBORA	Indeed. It was the 14th of February, a Thursday, and Anne Thorne, our maidservant, had contrived to dislocate her knee. I was not pleased to see she was not wearing her apron and I'm a stickler for proper dress, but when I picked it up it was all rolled up around a few twigs. A reverend's wife gains great experience of humankind and I know witchcraft when I see it, so I threw the twigs on the fire and lo and behold who should appear but Mrs Wenham herself, muttering some nonsense about having an errand from Ardeley Bury. Of course I made enquiries later and Ardeley Bury had never asked her to deliver any such message…

DEBORA is interrupted by some fuss around ANNE who is about to faint and is being held up by ARTHUR CHAUNCY.

DEBORA	And then Anne started acting most strangely…
POWELL	Thank you Mrs Gardiner. I think it would be more profitable to hear from the girl herself. Come forward Miss Thorne.
ARTHUR	She is not ready to speak my lord.
DEBORA	I would like to say my lord that in all my years in Walkern, I have known Jane Wenham to be nothing but a thief and a beggar and the one time she did our washing, my linen came back from her dirtier than it went.
POWELL	Thank you Mrs Gardiner. Thomas Adams.

ADAMS comes to the witness box.

POWELL	Mr Adams, you are a farmer…
ADAMS	Landowner, your honour. I have 50 acres around Walkern.
POWELL	Your evidence Mr Adams.
ADAMS	It was about three weeks before Christmas. I found Jane Wenham in my turnip field carrying away some of my turnips. I said she'd better put 'em down or she'd feel my fist. She said she'd had nothing to

	eat that day. I told her to clear off and she did. Well, on Christmas day morning one of my best sheep died. And when my shepherd cut it open we couldn't find one sign of illness upon its body.
BRAGGE	Christmas day you see. The Devil hates Christmas.
ADAMS	Nine or ten days after, another sheep died in an unaccountable manner and shortly after two more. And my shepherd said another sheep was taken strangely, skipping and standing on its head. But it's well now.
DEBORA	Like the pig!
POWELL	Do these ovine incidents have anything to do with Jane Wenham?
ADAMS	Well everyone knows she's a witch so I reckon if they were bewitched she's the one who did it.
POWELL	Thank you Mr Adams. Now, while we're on the subject of cursed animals, let us call Thomas Chapman. Mr Chapman?

CHAPMAN lurches up. He is horribly drunk.

POWELL	Mr Chapman. Tell the court why you named Mrs Wenham as a witch.
CHAPMAN	Hurh… not so pleased with yourself now are you Jane?
POWELL	What events led you to believe your cattle had been bewitched?
CHAPMAN	Not just my cows – my cow-man! Poor old Matthew – covered in shit! *(He laughs raucously and points at JANE.)* Used to be a fine figure of a woman. Wouldn't know it now, would you? Fine figure, but proud, gentlemen of the jairy… jury…. Shouldn't have been so stuck up, should you Jane? *(He leaves the witness box and lurches towards JANE.)* I only wanted a kiss. A lickle kiss. Gimme a kiss Jane. *(He leans towards her and then tries to spit at her. A sergeant pulls him away.)* You filthy hag!

He is about to vomit. The sergeant takes him out.

POWELL   Never mind. We have his deposition. For what it's worth. Now, let's hear from a more dainty creature. Miss Thorne. Are you ready now?

With fuss, ANNE is helped on to the witness stand.

POWELL   Good of you to join us Miss Thorne. Now, if you could give us a full account of what has happened to you in the past weeks.

DEBORA   Tell the judge Anne. Speak up.

ANNE   … I looked behind me and there was an old woman all muffled in a riding-hood I couldn't see her face and I had to run…

POWELL   From the beginning Miss Thorne…

ANNE   …She was telling me to run up White Hill but she was sticking pins all over me… she was on the other side of the hedge, the old woman and she put her hand through the hedge, it was black, a black hand, and… aah!

ANNE falls writhing on the floor. DEBORA, ARTHUR and BRAGGE gather round.

POWELL   What is this?

ARTHUR   One of her fits my lord.

ANNE yells, moans, writhes with convulsions.

POWELL   This is new. Gentlemen of the jury, in all my years of these trials I have never had a fit inside the court house before. What is the cure?

BRAGGE   Prayer my lord. With several hours of prayer we have been able to pull her through these attacks.

POWELL   Several hours? I was hoping to be out of here in time for dinner.

ARTHUR   Let her at the witch.

POWELL	What?
ARTHUR	Bring Wenham to her. That does it. Do you remember, the night she died?
POWELL	Who died?
BRAGGE	Anne Thorne. After the worst of her fits. She was cold, her pulse gone. Then someone brought Mrs Wenham into the room and immediately, this maid started up and flew at her.

ANNE's fit has subsided and she lies on the floor, apparently unconscious.

ARTHUR	Quick, have the witch brought over.
POWELL	Certainly not!
ARTHUR	Do you want the girl to die?
POWELL	Very well.

JANE is brought over to where ANNE lies. Everyone watches, hushed. Suddenly ANNE leaps up and slashes with her nails at JANE's face.

ANNE	So are you here again to torment me? I'll have your blood!
POWELL	Separate them!
ANNE	I'll tear you to pieces!

ANNE is dragged away and falls down again in a faint. JANE is taken back to the dock. Attempts are made to revive ANNE.

ARTHUR	She cannot speak my lord. But you have her information to Sir Henry.
POWELL	I had hoped the jury might have the benefit of hearing her own words but let it go. They have had entertainment instead. What a shame we will not hear from one with personal experience of being bewitched.

MARGARET STRETE pushes her way through to the witness stand.

MARGARET	She bewitched me!

POWELL   I see, miss…?

MARGARET   Margaret Strete your honour lordship sir. I was going to work. And there was an old woman by the side of the road.

POWELL   Was it Mrs Wenham?

MARGARET   I couldn't see her face, she wore a hood. I said 'Good morning'. And she said, 'Not such a good morning for you, Margaret'. And all of a sudden it happened.

ANNE interrupts with loud moaning.

POWELL   Reverends, back to your prayers it seems. Go on Miss Strete.

MARGARET   It was like my body was not my own. And my feet lifted off the ground. And I went up, and up and up. I was flying – she made me fly!

Murmurs from the crowd of 'bewitched, bewitched'.

POWELL   Did this old woman fly too?

MARGARET   She must have done. I went up and up until I was as high as the top of this oak tree…

ANNE   *(Moans)* This tree's all made of sticks…

MARGARET   *(Loudly)* I flew like a bird right over the tree.

POWELL   And did anyone else witness this remarkable occurrence?

MARGARET   No but I got proof.

She reaches into her apron pocket and pulls out a handful of rather withered leaves.

MARGARET   I picked these!

POWELL   A bunch of oak leaves does not constitute proof.

MARGARET   Not if they was ordinary leaves. But these are the leaves that grow at the top of the tree. I could only have picked them if I was flying!

Murmurs of assent and appreciation all round.

POWELL   How did you get down?

MARGARET   I landed with such a bump. I still got the bruise. Look…

She hitches up her skirts to show her thigh. Cheers and laughter from the crowd.

BRAGGE   Wenham flew my lord! Proof she's a witch!

POWELL   But not a hanging offence. I can assure you there's no law in England against flying.

MARGARET starts flapping her arms and running round.

POWELL   Sit down girl.

MARGARET   I cannot. She has control of my body!

ANNE moans louder.

BRAGGE   Cease your wicked designs on these innocent girls!

JANE   T'ain't me.

POWELL   Sit down Miss Strete! Take the weight off your wings.

MARGARET sits down, to much acclaim. ANNE's cries and moans get louder.

BRAGGE   We should pray. 'A Strong Tower' has been most effective.

The two clergymen kneel down beside her.

BRAGGE /
GARDINER   The name of the Lord is a strong tower, the righteous man runs into it and is safe…

POWELL   Reverend Bragge. I am calling you as a witness. Now.

BRAGGE takes the witness box.

POWELL   Reverend. What can you tell us?

BRAGGE   I chanced to pay a neighbourly visit to the Gardiners and Miss Thorne…

POWELL   Reverend Bragge. We have a very detailed deposition from Mrs Gardiner. Have you any new matter to add?

BRAGGE   New. Oh, I don't believe we've heard about the feathers.

POWELL   No, we've had no feathers yet.

BRAGGE   On Tuesday the 19th of February I called at the Rectory and Mrs Gardiner commented that in cases of bewitching, items are frequently found inside the victim's pillow. So she reached inside Anne's pillow and found a most curious object. I examined it scientifically…

POWELL   And it was…?

BRAGGE   I may describe it as a cake of feathers. It was circular, made of 32 feathers, with their quills towards the centre, set into some sort of viscous matter. I found inside it some hairs, black and grey, which I can say with confidence were cat hairs!

Murmurs in the crowd. ANNE moans louder and GARDINER steps up the prayer.

BRAGGE   And we found more of these objects over the next days. Five in all.

POWELL   I would greatly like to see an enchanted feather. Would you be so kind as to display one of these mysterious cakes Reverend Bragge?

BRAGGE   Well I haven't, er… They were burnt.

POWELL   All of them?

BRAGGE   Yes.
POWELL   Didn't you think to preserve one of them, scientifically?

BRAGGE	They, er, that is, it was generally agreed we should throw them into the fire and that would ease poor Anne's torments.
POWELL	And did it?

ANNE's wails grow louder and she starts to writhe again.

ARTHUR	Her torments will not cease while that woman lives!

Suddenly ANNE leaps up and points to the centre of the room.

ANNE	Cat!

The crowd gasps and shrinks back.

ANNE	It's staring at me. Stop it staring!
POWELL	Sit down Miss Thorne. There is no cat.
MARGARET	I seen cats. Cats with her face. *(She points to JANE)*

Cries of 'me too, me too'.

ANNE	*(To the cat)* Get away from me Jane, you shall not have me!
POWELL	Mrs Wenham is here in front of you.
ANNE	It is Jane. It comes in my room. It leaps on my bed and claws me…
ARTHUR	The cat is Wenham's familiar. She sends it out to do her work.
BRAGGE	She has wreaked terror in the village while locked up here in Hertford.
POWELL	Can't you bring your animal under control Mrs Wenham?
JANE	It's not me. I hate cats. Nasty creatures. Kill birds.
ARTHUR	Proof of her pact with the devil my lord!

POWELL   No doubt, if only I could see this invisible marvel. Let me get my glasses.

Laughter. He peers at the empty space.

POWELL   No, sadly, this wonder has not been revealed to me. Well, someone put a bowl of cream outside and perhaps we can be rid of it.

ARTHUR   I killed one of these demons with my bare hands!

POWELL   Your bare hands! A true Hercules.

ARTHUR   It was besieging the Rectory, clawing at the door. I have proof. My lord you wanted to see the bewitched feathers, see the demon itself!

He reaches into a bag and pulls out the stiff body of the dead cat, holding it up by its tail. Everyone recoils from the stench.

POWELL   Remarkable…

ARTHUR   Thank you.

POWELL   Gentlemen of the jury – would you care to examine the evidence? *(Pause)* I am sorry Mr Chauncy. It appears they do not. Perhaps we can have the bag placed in another room. How fortunate we are to have such potent evidence. Have we heard…?

ARTHUR   Oh God – Anne has a knife!

ANNE stands and tries to stab at her arm with a penknife.

POWELL   Restrain her!

GARDINER and ARTHUR grab her but she is flailing around with the knife.

DEBORA   This is not the first time…

POWELL   Take her outside.

DEBORA   Your honour, the Rectory has become a madhouse, you must put a stop to this.

By now, there is a hubbub of yelling and jeering, ANNE moaning and struggling, MARGARET shrieking.

POWELL   Silence! I say we will hear the evidence. Take that girl outside!

ANNE is taken outside. As she goes, SIR HENRY CHAUNCY enters. He is quiet and seems unwell, but his presence commands respect. He says nothing but bows to POWELL and shakes hands with the jury. The court calms down as he takes a seat.

POWELL   Elizabeth Field, if you will.

ELIZABETH comes nervously to the witness box.

POWELL   You have not made a deposition Mrs Field. I presume that means you have seen no extraordinary cats.

ELIZABETH   No your lordship.

POWELL   Nor flown.

ELIZABETH   No your lordship.

POWELL   But you have known Mrs Wenham many years. What would you like to tell the court?

ELIZABETH   Well sir. I was sitting with the wife of Richard Harvey sir, as she was very ill and like to die.

POWELL   I beg your pardon? When was this?

ELIZABETH   About twelve years ago last Christmas sir.

POWELL   Twelve years! If I wanted to hear about the Antiquities of Hertfordshire, I would read Sir Henry Chauncy's book.

ELIZABETH   It is to do with Jane sir. She was under Mrs Harvey's window and I heard her say, 'Why is this creature lingering on? Why don't they take her and hang her out of the way?' And I put my head out of the window and I said, 'Why don't they take you and hang you out of the way!' And then Jane said, 'Shut up, Elizabeth, my quarrel's not with you.' So, Mrs Harvey died that night. Then *(she starts to get upset)* a few days later Jane came round to my house and I was nursing this child. And Jane stroked his

	head. And the next week the baby fell ill for no reason and died. Just like Mrs Harvey.
POWELL	Are you saying Mrs Wenham bewitched the child?
ELIZABETH	I don't know. It happened like that.
POWELL	But you did not bring a complaint at the time?
ELIZABETH	I am a poor woman sir. I have no money for the law.
POWELL	And are you now suddenly grown rich?
ELIZABETH	No sir.
POWELL	Do you allege Jane Wenham killed the infant?
ELIZABETH	I don't know. I just thought I should speak.
POWELL	You speak but you seem to have no opinion.
DEBORA	Only a month ago she was telling us Jane saved her son.
POWELL	Is this true?
ELIZABETH	No. Yes.
POWELL	No or yes?
ELIZABETH	I did go to Jane for a remedy. But it was God who saved him.
POWELL	Are you claiming the accused also killed Mrs Harvey?
DEBORA	Everyone knows she hated the Harveys.
POWELL	Why?
DEBORA	Because when Wenham left her it was Richard Harvey took the message to the town crier in Hertford.
POWELL	What message?

DEBORA   Wenham had the town crier cry down his wife so everyone would know he had nothing more to do with her and no-one was to trust her with any credit because he wasn't going to pay her debts.

There is a general hum of agreement that this was so.

ADAMS   She's a beggar and a thief!

POWELL   Mrs Wenham. Stand up.

JANE stands. The jeering gets louder.

POWELL   What have you to say to these accusations?

JANE   I'm a clear woman sir.

POWELL   You confessed to being a witch.

JANE   They made me.

BRAGGE   She failed the Lord's Prayer test.

JANE   You know I know it!

POWELL   Mrs Wenham. No-one has spoken in your defence so you must speak for yourself. What have you to say?

JANE shrugs. The jeering continues.

POWELL   We have heard extraordinary accusations, going back years. Why do you think your neighbours have made these allegations?

JANE looks round the room, in the faces of all present. People grow quieter, expectantly.

POWELL   What do you say is the source of Anne Thorne's afflictions?

JANE snorts derisively.

POWELL   Do you not wish to say that you are a harmless woman who means no ill to anybody?

JANE says nothing.

POWELL   Mrs Wenham. If you have a tongue, use it!

There is silence. JANE stares at him stonily.

Sniggers from the crowd. POWELL is furious.

POWELL   Gentlemen of the jury. You have witnessed today some astonishing performances by persons whose talents are clearly wasted in the back lanes of Hertfordshire. You have seen a dismal show from the accused and an even worse one from her only confessed friend. However, you may ask yourselves whether you have heard anything that resembles truth, honesty and Christian charity and which does not stem from petty resentment and a fevered imagination. You may consider your verdict.

The jury do not retire but talk among themselves.

ARTHUR   Sir Henry says she is a witch. Whom will you believe?

POWELL   Mr Chauncy! You are not the judge appointed by the Crown. I have had enough of your ignorant interventions.

The hubbub in the courtroom grows, becoming increasingly hostile, mocking POWELL. The jury foreman stands.

POWELL   Sirs. Have you come to a decision?

FOREMAN   We have my lord.

POWELL   How do you find the accused?

FOREMAN   Guilty my lord.

The court erupts into cheers and yells.

POWELL   Silence! Jane Wenham. You have been found guilty of the charge of conversing with the devil. In the shape of a cat. The penalty by law is to be hanged until you are dead. You will be removed to Hertford town gaol until such time as the penalty is carried out. Clear the court.

SCENE 6

The gaol. Two weeks later. JANE sits in leg irons, dirtier and more ragged than ever. GEORGE enters and gives her a crust of bread. She eats it without complaining.

GEORGE   Cheer up Jane. Can't be long now.

JANE   It's already been three days… four?

GEORGE   It's been two weeks Jane.

She struggles to take this in.

JANE   Perhaps they've changed their mind.

GEORGE   They never change their mind. *(Pause)* Come on woman. Courage. It's the only way.

JANE   I was ready, after the trial. I tell you, if they'd hauled me out then and there and put the noose around my neck, I'd have laughed in their faces. They hated me for being a witch and I didn't care. But now they don't hate me enough to hang me.

GEORGE   I expect someone hasn't signed a chit somewhere.

JANE   I been planning what to do after I'm dead.

GEORGE   Oh yes?

JANE   Yes. I'm going to haunt them for the rest of their lives, Anne, Debora, that Bragge boy, Chapman. Heh heh. I didn't do nothing to them in life, but by God I will in death!

GEORGE laughs.

JANE   And when I go out to hang, and they're all watching, they'll know by the look in my eye that I shall come to get them and make their days a torture!

Pause.

JANE   But when's it going to be George?

GEORGE   What about your demon cats? Can't they tell you?

JANE	*(Laughs)* Are they still about?
GEORGE	So they say.
JANE	I saw a robin this morning. Perched between the bars there.
GEORGE	Was it sent by the Devil?
JANE	I don't reckon so. I was pleased to see it. Even though it means death. A robin in the house means a death to come.
GEORGE	This is the town gaol. We should have a whole colony of robins.
JANE	That's it you see. There's no correspondence there. Robins are full of life. It's a silly belief. Not useful. I always tried to be useful George. Ever since I learned from old Agnes, about plants and the law of similars. It was all there in a herbal she had. How things had a correspondence. Between the shape of a plant and a part of the body it could heal. God had made these herbs with a purpose. And dreams, Agnes said, had a pattern and a purpose, however daft they seemed in daylight. And she was right. The more people told me their dreams, the more patterns I saw. My first husband used to laugh at me. That's what mad folk do, he said, see causes that aren't there. Stop trying to understand what can't be understood, he said. What can't be helped.

Pause.

GEORGE	Should have listened to him, shouldn't you?

SCENE 7

A coffee house near Fleet Street. It is busy, both with well-dressed gentlemen and working men, all talking, drinking, reading newspapers. The proprietor, MRS WILLIS, is serving. Among the clientele are a TYPESETTER and a DYER. JOSEPH ADDISON, MP and writer, sits at one table. Authoritative and self-assured, he is surrounded by people who agree with his every word, apart from one, rival writer DANIEL DEFOE.

ADDISON …But listen, listen to this… *(He holds up a broadsheet newspaper and reads from it)* The Spectator, November the 12th, 1711. In this article I painted a charming portrait of an English village. But all is not well. Spiteful rumours have been circulating about one of the elderly residents, old Moll White. *(He reads)* 'There is scarce a village in England that has not a Moll White in it. When an old woman begins to doat and grow chargeable to the parish, she is generally turned into a witch and fills the whole country with imaginary distempers and terrifying dreams.' … Well? November 1711! I wrote that more than six months ago! Can I not scry the future? Who is this Jane Wenham but another Moll White?

DEFOE Is diabolic sorcery now a subject for fun in your little rag?

ADDISON You're no fool Defoe. How can you believe in witches?

DEFOE I know nothing about witches but I know when the Devil is at work.

ADDISON The only ones at work here are the Tories. You're supporting the High Church mob. Look up, the skies are full of high-flying clergymen! And I thought you were a sober non-conformist Daniel.

REV HUTCHINSON enters. He looks around and speaks to MRS WILLIS.

HUTCHS'N Excuse me Madam. I am looking for Mr Addison MP?

MRS WILLIS That's him – holding court over there.

HUTCHS'N Mr Addison? Francis Hutchinson at your service sir. I wrote to you.

ADDISON   You did indeed. Take a seat Reverend. Welcome to our cause.

HUTCHS'N   It has been a cause of mine for many years sir. This Wenham business has brought matters to a head. Were you at the trial?

ADDISON   Matters of Parliament detained me you know.

HUTCHS'N   I was there. Sir, the dangers were on display for all to see. The crowd, the shrieking girls. The accused herself could say nothing, transfixed like a rabbit before a weasel. If the jury had returned a verdict they disliked, the crowd would have been out on the streets. Discovering witchcraft is just an excuse for a mob!

ADDISON   Popular entertainment – nothing more.

DEFOE   Aren't you a parson?

HUTCHS'N   Actually I have just been appointed a Queen's Chaplain, by Her Majesty's grace.

DEFOE   So, you believe in God but not in the Devil? All is goodness in your world is it? No evil, no misery, no disease?

HUTCHS'N   I do not say that. Belief in good and bad spirits is an essential part of every Christian's faith. But imaginary communications with these spirits have given rise to the worst corruptions of religion and perversions of justice!

ADDISON   Daniel, you don't believe all this pins and feathers stuff.

DEFOE   I'm not saying whether there was witchcraft in this particular case, but pacts are made with the Devil – it is possible…

ADDISON   Well if I were a starving old woman who met the Devil, I wouldn't bother with sticking pins in silly ninnies, I'd ask for a good leg of ham!

Laughter all round.

Commotion as FRANCIS BRAGGE enters, followed by EDWARD CURLL and a young lad, TOM, carrying a stack of pamphlets.

ADDISON   Bragge! The literary phenomenon!

MRS WILLIS Not more pamphlets…

BRAGGE   My new publication…

TOM   Hot from the presses gentlemen, be the first to read it. Thruppence to you sir.

DYER   Is it the same lies as the first one?

BRAGGE   The first one is running into a third edition now, my man. Mr Curll is very pleased, aren't you Curll?

CURLL   Ain't you got no beer?

MRS WILLIS This is a coffee house Ned Curll.

DYER   I've never read such trash. *(He produces a tattered copy)* Right from the title – 'A Full and Impartial Account of the Discovery of Sorcery and Witchcraft Practis'd by Jane Wenham …'. Impartial? You were the one who called her a witch from the start.

BRAGGE   I was instrumental in uncovering her devilish practices, yes…

DYER   Making a girl with a bad knee jump over gates? Oooh… evil stalks the land.

ADDISON   It's true. The whole business is so milk-and-water. Where is that other pamphlet? *(Someone hands him a different pamphlet and he finds a page in it)* This author – Mr… Anonymous – says he reads in the books of demonography, 'that the Devil at their Sabbath meetings gives them the liver of an unbaptised child… he likewise sucks the blood of the left foot of the witch…' Did we get any of that in Walkern? Did Jane Wenham eat the liver of a child? Most disappointing.

BRAGGE	All sorts of scoffers and atheists have jumped into print, but I have my answers in this new pamphlet. Mr Curll believes it will sell as many as the first.
DYER	Just because people buy your pamphlets don't mean they agree with you.
BRAGGE	I am exposing you Whigs, Mr Addison. Your party has been supporting Wenham because she says she was prosecuted out of spite, for going to chapel meetings.
ADDISON	Is Wenham one of yours Defoe?
DEFOE	Do you mean a dissenter?
MRS WILLIS	Chapel goers – always seeing visions!
DEFOE	Some people are moved by the spirit at meetings. It does not make them witches. Just the opposite.
HUTCHS'N	But it is the first step down a dangerous road Mr Defoe. We start with enthusiasts, Quakers and the like and we end up with crazed prophets claiming the end of the world is nigh.
ADDISON	Daniel has never been moved by any spirit, except the urge to earn a guinea.
DEFOE	You take lightly a very serious subject Mr Hutchinson.
HUTCHS'N	I take it very seriously when innocent people are losing their lives. How many miserable creatures have been hanged or burned as witches, and not just here in England? All on account of, as I explain in my book, one ill-translated text of scripture…
BRAGGE	'Thou shalt not suffer a witch to live,' Exodus 22, verse 18.
HUTCHS'N	Did they each you nothing at Cambridge Mr Bragge? 'Witch' is a complete mistranslation of the Hebrew. Moses was condemning frauds and soothsayers.

BRAGGE	Are you some expert in theology sir?
DYER	He's a Queen's chaplain mate.
CURLL	Bible says witch. Witch is what they are.
TYPESETTR	There's no witches. Only serving girls and old biddies believe that.
DYER	Don't let Mrs Willis hear you!
MRS WILLIS	Any cheek and I'll turn you into a cat!

Jeers of 'a cat', 'I can see it' etc.

ADDISON	Where is Arthur Chauncy – that valiant scourge of cats!
BRAGGE	It is not amusing gentlemen when the lives of two young women are still in danger. Anne Thorne is tormented by fits and Margaret Strete has tried to drown herself.
ADDISON	I thought the charms were broken once the witch was convicted.
BRAGGE	Once she is hanged.
TYPESETTR	One of these pamphlets is written by a physician. He reckons Anne Thorne is suffering from mania. And he says belief in witchcraft is Papist superstition.
DEFOE	Oh yes, throw 'Papist' at anyone you disagree with.
BRAGGE	The Reverend Gardiner and I are accused of performing some Papist exorcism. Is the Book of Common Prayer Romish superstition now?
HUTCHS'N	It is not prayer but your credulous use of it.
BRAGGE	Sir, if you read my new pamphlet…
TOM	Only thruppence sirs… Get the new Bragge. 'Witchcraft further display'd…'

ADDISON	We are winning the battle of the pamphlets Bragge. How many have you got supporting you? Daniel?
DEFOE	I have not written any.
ADDISON	Well that makes a change. Ah yes, there is, 'The belief of witchcraft vindicated…'.
BRAGGE	Makes some good arguments.
MRS WILLIS	Amazingly tedious.
ADDISON	Whereas the publications attacking yours are mounting up thick and fast Bragge. 'The Case of the Hertfordshire Witchcraft Considered.'
BRAGGE	Atheistical and misconceived.
TYPESETTR	See? If you don't believe in witches they say you don't believe in God!
HUTCHS'N	Our faith must be grounded in something more than belief in cats with human faces.

Another printer's boy, HARRY, enters, carrying a stack of pamphlets.

HARRY	Gentlemen – just now off the presses. 'A Full Confutation of Witchcraft'.
DYER	*(Takes pamphlet)* 'In which the modern notions of witches are overthrown.'
HARRY	Thruppence to you sir.
TOM	'Witchcraft further display'd'. Read the true story! Devil cats and dogs!
HARRY	What dogs?
TOM	Demon dogs.
HARRY	Liar!
TOM	'Strue! It's in the pamphlet!

HARRY	Your pamphlets? They're only good for wiping your arse.
TOM	I'll wipe your arse…

He hits out at the other lad. A fight ensues. Customers try to separate them, or cheer them on. The fight spreads. One man tears up Bragge's new pamphlet.

DYER	Typical Tory lies!
DEFOE	Atheist!
DYER	Party hack… *(Aims a blow at him)*
CURLL	Whigs! Think you know it all…
TYPESETTR	Better than being a Tory fool…

The boys are tussling on the floor. Men are arguing and shoving.

MRS WILLIS Gentlemen, please…

The coffee house descends into mayhem.

SCENE 8

The gaol. JANE is no longer in irons but is very weak and can barely move. GEORGE crouches beside her with a bowl and is trying to feed her from a spoon.

JANE	…Give…

She turns her head aside when he puts the spoon to her mouth.

GEORGE	Come on Jane. Just a little… bread and milk Jane… come on.
JANE	…Give us this day…

She breaks off, coughing badly.

GEORGE	Just a spoonful… do you good.

He manages to get a spoonful down her.

JANE	Give us… no not…

GEORGE	And again…
JANE	Not into no… no
GEORGE	Come on Jane.
JANE	No… not into no… Our Father…
GEORGE	Don't die now Jane. Judge Powell has gone to the Queen.
JANE	… Who art in heaven…
GEORGE	Get a pardon for you Jane…
JANE	… temptation…
GEORGE	A royal pardon. Come on Jane… come on.

She weeps.

SCENE 9

Three years later. April 1715. JANE WENHAM's cottage on the Cowper estate, west of Hertford.
ELIZABETH enters. She looks tired. She carries a basket.

JANE enters, also carrying a basket. She is neatly dressed, in plain but clean clothes.

JANE	What are you doing here?
ELIZABETH	I wanted to see how you were.
JANE	It's a two mile walk here from Old Cross. It'll kill you.
ELIZABETH	I'm alright. The carter let Ned drive today. You should've seen him, sitting up there.
JANE	I hadn't heard from you.
ELIZABETH	We haven't been to Hertford market for months.
JANE	I didn't know if you'd got through the winter.

ELIZABETH	What are you picking?
JANE	Sorrel. The cook's doing trout in sorrel sauce for her Ladyship. They have it in the garden but wild is better, sharper.
ELIZABETH	Trout.
JANE	His Lordship is very proud of his trout river.
ELIZABETH	They say the Mimram is pretty.
JANE	It's not as nice as the Beane. What news then?
ELIZABETH	Sir Henry is not well. Last time I saw him he looked old.
JANE	He is old.
ELIZABETH	I thought he would be there forever, like the church tower.
JANE	Huh.
ELIZABETH	Anne Thorne, Anne Burville I mean, has had her third. Three in less than three years Jane! She is a rag of a girl now.

ELIZABETH coughs, badly.

ELIZABETH	I won't stay.
JANE	Wait.

She goes off and brings back something wrapped in a cloth.

JANE	Leftover from the leg of lamb they had on Sunday. There's bread in there too.
ELIZABETH	Jane it's not what I came for.
JANE	Cook gives me more than I can eat. Go on. Ned will like it.
ELIZABETH	Thank you Jane. Good bye.

She puts the food in her basket and exits. JANE sits and picks through the sorrel leaves.

FRANCIS HUTCHINSON enters.

HUTCHS'N   Mrs Wenham?

JANE stands, wary.

HUTCHS'N   Mrs Wenham. *(He goes to her confidently and shakes her hand)* Francis Hutchinson, at your service.

JANE   Reverend.

HUTCHS'N   What have you been gathering?

JANE   It's only for the kitchen sir. Sorrel. And some Jack-in-the-Hedge. Lady Cowper likes it in a salad.

HUTCHS'N   The Cowpers always have a fine table.

JANE   I do a lot for the cook. I don't have to but I like to. He says, Jane, I know you'll always bring me good stuff. Because I know where to look.

HUTCHS'N   It's a remarkable skill.

JANE   Are you a friend of the Cowpers sir?

HUTCHS'N   Yes.

JANE   They gave me this cottage. I don't know why they did.

HUTCHS'N   Because it was not safe for you to go back to Walkern.

JANE   I don't have to help the cook. They said, you don't have to do anything, you're not a servant. But I like to keep busy.

HUTCHS'N   That's good.

JANE   I go to St Mary's every Sunday sir. The vicar knows me.

HUTCHS'N	So I hear.
JANE	I had never heard of Lord Cowper. I didn't say so. I thought perhaps he was a friend of Sir Henry's?
HUTCHS'N	Not exactly. He is a friend of… friends of yours.
JANE	I got no friends sir. You don't know who I am.
HUTCHS'N	I know who you are. I was there at your trial.
JANE	Were you? Beg pardon sir. I can't remember anything of it.
HUTCHS'N	Are you happy here?
JANE	It is a very nice cottage, sir. I miss my river.
HUTCHS'N	Have you many visitors?
JANE	They used to come over from town to gawp at me but the bailiff chased 'em away.
HUTCHS'N	It is so very peaceful here, after London. Peace is the greatest human blessing, don't you think?

He starts writing in his notebook.

HUTCHS'N	Excuse me while I make a few notes. My impressions – of this delightful countryside, your cottage. You. *(Pause)* I am writing a book.
JANE	Oh.
HUTCHS'N	In actual fact I have already written it. 'An Historical Essay Concerning Witchcraft'. There was much useful material at your trial. I am just waiting for all the party debate to die down before I publish. In my position I must steer clear of politics.
JANE	Are you important then sir?
HUTCHS'N	Well I am a chaplain to the new King George. And, er, I am in line to be a bishop. I shall be going to Ireland. There is much work to be done there.

JANE	Oh.
HUTCHS'N	But there is much work to be done here in England. So much ignorance. Mrs Wenham, we live in a world of harmony and order, spoilt only by ourselves. The vast stretch of space is filled with sun and moon and a thousand stars in their mystic dance. So just, so strange, everything rapid, yet beautiful and unconfused. Newton's vision of the universe. That is God's order.

Pause. JANE goes back to picking through her herbs.

HUTCHS'N	Ideally the witchcraft act should be repealed. But until it is, in trials such as yours, the judiciary should have a set of laws to follow, according to firm scientific principles. I set out these laws in my book, all of them rooted in scripture. Granted, there have been no witchcraft trials since yours. But there could be – superstition is never far off! Indeed it is encouraged by these cheap publications which circulate, giving an exaggerated account of witchcraft cases in unnecessary detail.
JANE	Am I in one?
HUTCHS'N	Of course. I have a collection of 94 pamphlets now, about cases from all over the country, and even New England. The correspondences between events are striking. Always the same stories of pins and straw. Remarkable, don't you think?
JANE	You know more about it than me sir.
HUTCHS'N	The same so-called proofs of a witch, like the inability to say the Lord's Prayer.
JANE	It is unjust.
HUTCHS'N	I agree.
JANE	Because I knew it! I known it all my life. Our Father which art in heaven…
HUTCHS'N	No no, Mrs Wenham… I am confident you know it.

JANE   I didn't do nothing.

HUTCHS'N   I believe you Mrs Wenham. So does Lord Cowper. He acted out of pity for you as a victim of injustice.

JANE   I couldn't do nothing. And I couldn't say nothing. They'd made up their minds.

HUTCHS'N   I was there in court Mrs Wenham. I saw the pitiable state you were in.

JANE   And when I tried to say it, I couldn't. The words were flying about my head. They did something to my mouth. My mouth was going to be the death of me. And I thought – so let it be the death of me. So I kept quiet.

HUTCHS'N   Lord Justice Powell understood your plight. He went to the Queen himself to obtain your pardon.

JANE   I never saw him after.

HUTCHS'N   He is retired now.

JANE   Our Father
                Which art in heaven
                Hallowed be thy name.
                Thy kingdom come
                Thy will be done… *(she hesitates)* Let me try again.

HUTCHS'N   It is alright Mrs Wenham.

JANE   I know it. It is something I know! Our Father…

HUTCHS'N   You do not need to say it…

JANE   *(Forceful)* I can say it. Listen to me!

                Our Father
                Which art in heaven
                Hallowed be thy name.
                Thy kingdom come
                Thy will be done
                On earth as it is in heaven.
                Give us this day our daily bread.
                And forgive us our trespasses

>   As we forgive them that trespass against us.
>   And lead us not into temptation.
>   But deliver us from evil.
>   For thine is the kingdom, and the power, and the glory
>   For ever and ever
>   Amen.

She stands, triumphant, powerful.

HUTCHINSON, unnerved, picks up his notebook.

HUTCHS'N	God bless you Mrs Wenham. You are, er, a simple and pious woman. When I publish my book the whole country will be fully convinced of your innocence.
JANE	Thank you sir.
HUTCHS'N	It has been most interesting to meet you. Good day.

He shakes her hand and exits.

JANE sits down and sorts through her basket.

A teenaged girl, MARY, enters. She hangs around nervously. When JANE does not acknowledge her, she comes a little nearer.

MARY	Mother?
JANE	Go away.
MARY	Mother Jane?
JANE	I ain't your mother.
MARY	Has he gone? *(Pause)* I need your help.
JANE	I can't help. Go home.
MARY	No I really do. I can pay.
JANE	I don't need money.
MARY	They say you know things.
JANE	Not me.

MARY	You do. I heard you say that spell. I was amazed.
JANE	It's not a spell, it's a prayer.

JANE stands up and looks at MARY.

JANE	What do you want? Let me guess. You're young, you didn't sleep last night. A love potion.
MARY	*(Mutters)* Too late for that.

Pause.

JANE	How many months?
MARY	Two I think.
JANE	Two, what's that? It might not stay.
MARY	I can't take the risk.
JANE	Tell your mother. She'll beat you but after that it'll be alright.
MARY	She's dead. Please Mrs Wenham. I know you know.
JANE	I don't know nothing. You shouldn't have come here.
MARY	Nobody saw me. Please. I shall lose my post at the house. Then we won't have any money coming in. I got four little brothers and sisters and my dad's been struck. He can't move. We feed him bread and milk. Please. I can't lose this position.

Pause.

JANE	Was he a nice looking boy?
MARY	Yes.
JANE	Be a nice looking baby. Marry him and have done with it.
MARY	He's gone. You're the only one who can help me.

Pause.

JANE: I don't keep the stuff with me. But I know where to find it. Hm, pennyroyal… Come back in three days. And don't tell no-one.

MARY: 'Course not.

JANE: It is a sin.

MARY: I know. I shall answer to God for it. I'm not afraid.

JANE: Neither am I.

MARY leaves.

JANE picks up her basket and starts humming to herself.

THE END

By Kate Miller, Emma Blowers and
Erin Thompson

Seeing it Through began as a collaborative project by writers Kate Miller, Emma Blowers and Erin Thompson to mark the centenary of the First World War. From the outset it was intended that the play would bring to the stage the words, actions and feelings of local people who lived through this historical event, as recorded in newspapers, reports and memoirs.

The small cast list of *Seeing it Through* belies the innumerable characters whose shared stories interweave through four years of international conflict covered in this two-act play. Expediency necessitated the cutting or combining of many more stories, which were set aside to be shared as part of the community history displays intended to accompany the production. The collaboration of the original cast of five actors, led by Director Richard Syms, was vital in choreographing a division of roles that successfully incorporated numerous character changes. Musical Director Christina Raven's score and vocal pieces created a soundscape which ranged from intimate interludes to epic episodes such as the Hertford Zeppelin Raid of 1915.

The original production was staged at Hertford Theatre in 2014. The multi-venue tour in 2016 took the Pins and Feathers cast, crew, plus the Heritage Lottery funded community history project team to local venues across East Hertfordshire. This achieved the writers' aim of sharing a significant chapter of local history in settings the characters featured would have known well and where some of their names, and many they loved, continue to be commemorated on memorial crosses, plaques and rolls of honour.

Inscribed on to the War Memorial at Thundridge's St Mary's Church are dozens of names and the words: 'All you who pass never forget that these men gave up their lives that you might enjoy your heritage'. *Seeing it Through* dramatically brings to life many stories of those men, women and children who found themselves on the home front in Hertford, Ware and the surrounding villages during The First World War; its themes of community, duty, lost innocence and personal sacrifice in the face of adversity are timeless and universal. We must not forget them.

Emma Blowers, co-writer and local historian.

Seeing It Through was first performed at Hertford Theatre in November 2014, with the following cast. All the actors took multiple roles, with the main ones as follows:

MERCURY	Richard Syms
CLAUD SWEENEY	Catherine Forrester
EMILY WILKES	Catherine Forrester
LOUISA PULLER	Catherine Forrester
ALFRED BURT	Catherine Forrester
W E JOHNS	Robert Madeley
MAJOR KINMAN	Robert Madeley
PEMBERTON-BILLING	Robert Madeley
ANNIE SWAN	Toni Brooks
ELIZABETH SWEENEY	Toni Brooks
JENNY MASON	Toni Brooks
GROCER	Stephen Scales
LADY SALISBURY	Stephen Scales
WILLIAM GRAVESON	Stephen Scales
ALBERT HAWKES	Christina Raven

Director	Richard Syms
Musical Director	Christina Raven

The touring production was first performed at Place House, Ware, on 8 October 2016. The creative team was the same, except for the following roles:

W E JOHNS	Darren Machin
MAJOR KINMAN	Darren Machin
PEMBERTON-BILLING	Darren Machin
GROCER	Ken Boyter
LADY SALISBURY	Ken Boyter
WILLIAM GRAVESON	Ken Boyter

ACT 1

Rumour grows. Excitement and anxiety. 'It's war'. 'There's going to be a war'. 'It will never happen'. 'Germany's going to invade'. 'It won't.' 'It's war... it's war...'

The voice of the HERTFORDSHIRE MERCURY newspaper is heard.

MERCURY   August. 1914. War with Germany is declared. Our duty as the leading nation in the path of progress is clear. Much as we deplore the war, it is one of self-preservation, calling for all those qualities of unity, bulldog tenacity and valour which have given us the victory in the past.

CLAUD SWEENEY, a 17 year old Scout steps out. He is in his uniform, carrying a stave.

SWEENEY   Claud Sweeney. Patrol leader, Ware Scouts. We were in the middle of camp up by Cromer windmill when the news came. And I thought, it's August. The Territorials C Company are on their annual camp at Ashridge. The Hertford Grammar boys are stuck on Officer Training Corps camp somewhere in the midlands. It's just us Boy Scouts here to protect the town. And we're ready.

MERCURY   We know that the war is none of our seeking, but has been deliberately forced upon us, and we will go forward with quiet confidence that God will defend the right.

W E (Bill) JOHNS steps forward.

W E JOHNS   Bill Johns. Captain WE Johns as my readers know me, creator of Biggles. As a boy in Hertford I had dreamed of being a soldier. At the Grammar School I had slogged through the head's – Major Kinman's – weekly drill parades in his beloved school cadet corps. Most of the boys thought it was a silly game. They couldn't guess that within a few years most of them would be doing these things in grim earnest on the fields of Flanders, or that before the war was over nearly a third of them...

MERCURY   This is the time for a display of all that is best in our national character.

A grocer's shop. ELIZABETH SWEENEY (CLAUD's mother) and EMILY WILKES are shopping.

ELIZABETH How much?!

GROCER Circumstances utterly beyond my control...

ELIZABETH You're telling me a loaf that cost sevenpence ha'penny last week is now ninepence?

GROCER Madam, yesterday the demand for goods in one day equalled the usual demand for a week...

A snooty BUTLER enters and presents a piece of paper to the GROCER.

BUTLER Her ladyship's order...

EMILY Oi, We were here first.

GROCER *(Unfolding enormously long list)* I'll see to it.

BUTLER Her ladyship wants it now. She has sent me down with the motor.

ELIZABETH It's people like this pushing up prices. Not everyone can afford to buy the whole shop in one go!

GROCER I can't, sir, really. I've got an order from the military for provisions and you can't get a cask of butter now for love nor money.

BUTLER I'm sure her ladyship can shop elsewhere. *(He leaves)*

EMILY There was a riot in Hitchin outside the bakers. Lad got a broken jaw, I heard. And the war's only been going a week. It's not like there's anything happening.

MERCURY Tuesday 18th August 1914. Herbert Clark, aged 17, of Burr's Green farm, near Chapmore End, was a porter for Great Eastern Railways. He was working at Felixstowe, near the docks.

CLARK wheels up his bike. Two nervous sentries are on guard.

SENTRY 1   Halt.

CLARK sighs and stops.

SENTRY 1   Who goes there? *(SENTRY 2 sniggers)* Shut up. Friend or foe?

CLARK   Friend.

SENTRY 1   Identify yourself.

CLARK   Clark. Eastern Railways. Come on, I want to get to bed. *(Pushes his bike)*

SENTRY 1   Halt or I fire. Show your pass.

CLARK   Oh come on…

SENTRY 1   I will. Hands up.

CLARK puts one hand up but holds the bike with the other.

SENTRY 2   It's a German spy.

CLARK   I'm going home.

SENTRY 1   *(Panicking)* Don't come any further!

CLARK   Stupid tin soldiers. *(Pushes bike)*

Sentry shoots. CLARK falls. The two go to his body.

SENTRY 2   *(Thrilled)* Got him. Got us a spy.

MERCURY   At the inquest the doctor reported that Mr Herbert Clark was admitted to the Pier Hotel military hospital, suffering from a bullet wound and bayonet thrust. The sentries said they could not recall using their bayonets. Mr Clark's funeral was held in Felixstowe and attended by Lord Salisbury in person. Officers from the Third Battalion North Lancashire Regiment were there and the soldiers stood to attention outside the church during the service.

Hymn.

MERCURY	Stirring scenes in Hertford. Mobilisation of county's forces.
ADVERT	At war!
MERCURY	As the headquarters of the 4th Beds regiment, the Territorials and the Yeomanry, Hertford presents the appearance of an armed camp.
ADVERT	At war! Drury Brothers has declared war on prices! While everything else is up, we have determined clothing shall be cheaper!
MERCURY	In Ware, the 1st Herts C Company assembled at the Drill Hall. Captain Henry Page Croft, the Commanding Officer, led them, mounted on a splendid charger. The drum and fife band struck up a lively selection, and the men headed for the barracks at Hertford. After parading at Hartham, the company marched through crowded streets to All Saints church, to lodge the Regiment's colours. Then the advance guard left.

ELIZABETH and her son CLAUD. He is now in army uniform.

ELIZABETH	What do you think you're doing?
SWEENEY	We're all going Mum. Ware boys are all together in this.
ELIZABETH	They won't let you. You're only 17.
SWEENEY	They are letting me. They know how old I am and they know I'm ready.
ELIZABETH	You're not a soldier Claud.
SWEENEY	I'm as good as a soldier. All those hours we've put in at the Drill Hall and down the rifle range – what was it for, if not for this? It's wonderful Mum. I'm going to serve my country and you're going to be proud of me.

He hugs her and leaves.

W E JOHNS	What boy didn't want to be a soldier? Soldiers were gods. I had seen them as a child. When troops went overseas they marched through cheering crowds, bands playing, colours flying. We boys marched with them to the railway station and yelled our heads off as the train steamed out, whistle screaming and fog signals thundering under the wheels. Of course when I left the grammar I didn't become a soldier. I became a sanitary inspector. In Norfolk. *(sighs)* But I did join the territorials. Now war is here and I am private no. 74451 in the King's Own Royal Regiment, the Norfolk Yeomanry. I have a horse called Pistol.

ANNIE SWAN comes forward.

ANNIE	Annie Swan. I'm a journalist and novelist, with something of a name in the literary world. Of course in Hertford my name is my husband's name. I'm Mrs Burnett Smith. My husband Jim is a GP here and on the town council – Mayor in fact, one year. We came to Hertford from Hampstead in 1908 because… well to be honest Hampstead life had proved rather a drain on our expenses. In the English county town, I discovered, the lines of demarcation are rigidly drawn. County does not mix with town, professional people with shopkeepers, church with chapel and so on, through all the minor grades. I heard a Hertford woman say: 'It is a pity one can't know doctors socially. Some of them are really quite nice.' As for a woman who writes books or speaks at meetings, she is a freak. But now it is wartime. What is a woman to do? A lot of people know the answer to that question, of course. Lady Salisbury for one…

LADY SALISBURY comes forward. She is very grand. Attended by an eager news reporter.

LADY S	Let me explain the organisation proposed in connection with needlework throughout the county…
REPORTER	A meeting of county people connected with the Voluntary Aid Detachment, the British Red Cross

	and the Hertfordshire Needlework Guild was held at Lady Salisbury's London town house…
LADY S	The object must be to get clothes made as quickly as possible. The Guild Secretary will send out patterns of the articles to be made.
REPORTER	Among those present were Lady Florence Cecil, the Countess of Verulam, Lady Faudel Phillips, the Earl and Countess of Lytton, the Honourable Mrs Abel Smith…
LADY S	The winter is before us and we must be prepared for the war lasting at least six months.
REPORTER	… The Honourable Mrs Reginald Smith, the Countess of Essex, the Countess of Cavan, The Countess of Strafford, Mrs Brodie Henderson, Mrs Longman…
LADY S	Shirts must be our priority. I have put out a call for flannel which I am sure will be answered.
MERCURY	Last week one thousand five hundred soldiers from the Gloucester and Warwickshire regiments were billeted in Port Vale and Bengeo.

On Bengeo Street. A young mother, MAUD, is talking to a Gloucester sergeant and a young corporal.

MAUD	How much?
SERGEANT	Three shillings fourpence ha'penny per man.
MAUD	Ooh.
SERGEANT	You to supply three meals a day and a bed.
MAUD	Right. *(Gives him a saucy look)*
SERGEANT	His own bed Mam. What about this house here then?
CORPORAL	No one at home sarge.

MAUD	Don't you believe it. She's hiding. Doesn't want your boys.
SERGEANT	What?
MAUD	Look, she's peeking out behind that curtain. Miserable old bat. And her with one of the biggest houses in Bengeo! She's got six bedrooms and nothing in 'em but dust. I've got two and I've got four kids and all.
CORPORAL	Lady at Ivy Lodge says she's happy to serve her country but she can only take an officer.
SERGEANT	She'll get who she's given.
MAUD	Can I have an officer?
SERGEANT	There's not enough to go round Mam.
CORPORAL	I'm a corporal. *(She smiles at him)*
SERGEANT	Where's your husband?
MAUD	At sea.
SERGEANT	Be gentle with him. He's not used to the town. More sheep than people where he's from.
CORPORAL	Hope you've got a decent bed Missus. I'm done in. Been on the road for two months non-stop.
SERGEANT	Two weeks yer chump.
MAUD	How did it take you two weeks?
SERGEANT	We came the long way. It hardens up the lads' marching feet. Three nights here and next stop…
CORPORAL	*(Grins)* France!
ANNIE	The panicky atmosphere of those first weeks was indescribable. The bogey was German invasion, which was reported to be imminent, sometimes actually to have materialised, at every vulnerable

spot. As a newcomer to the area, I was a little surprised to find that there really were Germans on our doorstep – a whole colony in fact, in a large house called Libury Hall, near Little Munden. What's more, they had been there for 14 years, attracting little attention. Until now.

Libury Hall. A POLICEMAN interviews the manager, HERR MÜLLER.

POLICE	Now then Mr Muller.
MÜLLER	*(Pronounces umlaut)* Müller.
POLICE	You are the manager of this, er, establishment.
MÜLLER	*(Proudly)* An industrial farm colony run on Christian principles. Set up by our generous patrons, Baron Brunno Schroeder and his brother, to provide work and shelter for destitute German-speaking men.
POLICE	You understand there will now be a permanent police presence at Libury Hall.
MÜLLER	You are our guests.
POLICE	62 of your chaps have already absconded.
MÜLLER	Absconded? They were free to leave.
POLICE	Well, they're now prisoners of war. So you don't want that to happen again.
MÜLLER	Officer, our aim has always been to help men earn enough money to return to their homeland. You cannot blame them for trying. We have a number of permanent residents.
POLICE	Make sure they don't leave.
MÜLLER	Most of them are over 80.
POLICE	And what exactly do you do here?
MÜLLER	We grow fruit. And bottle it.

POLICE	Hmph. I am informed by the Home Office you can expect to receive 300 German and Austrian married men of the respectable artisan type. Not troublemakers, just lost their job.
MÜLLER	Why?
POLICE	Because they're German. Many of them are married to English women I believe. Now, you have a 25 acre meadow – over there?
MÜLLER	Yes there.
POLICE	Which has been identified as a suitable site for a concentration camp for one thousand Germans and Austrians who have been prevented from returning home and will be interned as prisoners of war. This camp will be under military control and you will provide employment for the prisoners for the duration. Understood?
MÜLLER	Yes officer. But… I'm not sure we can grow that much fruit.

German folk song.

LOUISA PULLER and ANNIE SWAN come forward.

LOUISA	Louisa Puller, one of the Pullers at Youngsbury. I'm Secretary of the East Herts Women's Suffrage Society. Annie is the chairman – we're a jolly crew. Anyway, as soon as the war broke out we all agreed that the vote was the least of our worries now and we would use the association's organisation to do – whatever needed to be done. One of the first pressing things was to help the Belgians who fled to England when the Germans invaded their country. 200,000 crossed the Channel in four weeks.
ANNIE	I was Chairman of the Hertford Refugees Committee so I went to Alexandra Palace, where hundreds were waiting to be sorted out and sent to their various destinations. They huddled in groups under the vast dome of the Alexandra Palace. I talked to a ship's pilot who had brought 88 refugees from Ostend in a boat built for 15 passengers. Many

	families were incomplete. One stricken father and mother told me of their daughter Yvonne, young and pretty, who had been unfortunate enough to attract the attention of the German High Command. They expected never to see her again.
MERCURY	A regrettable incident. At the Territorials training camp, Mr AJ Ketterer, son of the late Mr C Ketterer, jeweller in Ware, was accused by some of the Bishops Stortford and Sawbridgeworth half of the Company of being a German spy and he was court martialled. Several Ware men were called on to identify him and, Mr Ketterer being so well known and respected, an apology was offered by the officer commanding. Nevertheless, a very unpleasant feeling has been created at the stigma on him. We can affirm that Mr Ketterer is a British subject and comes of a highly respected family known for many miles around.
EMILY	Spies! But we've always taken our clocks to Ketterers to be mended!
ELIZABETH	You don't know who to trust do you.
EMILY	Have you heard from Claud? He must be in France by now!
ELIZABETH	No. Bury St Edmunds.
EMILY	Bury St Edmunds? But. But that's further away from France than here.
ELIZABETH	I know. Oh Emily. Now my husband's talking of joining up.
EMILY	No.
ELIZABETH	I told him he was too old and he hit the roof. It's only made him more determined. What am I going to do?
EMILY	You're supposed to wave 'em off with a cheery smile Elizabeth. Everyone says so.

MERCURY	World's record battle at Verdun. Outcome undecided after a fortnight's duration. A patriotic meeting was held in Braughing and men were called to help the war effort by practising rifle shooting on a Sunday afternoon, like the English archers who won the battle of Crecy by practising at the butts after church.
W E JOHNS	I was expecting to go to France but we wound up in the trenches at Gallipoli, and then Salonika. It was a living horror. I learnt something about war. Take a million men and ask them if they want to leave their homes to fight, perhaps die. Not one will answer 'yes'. Yet when the time comes, they will go, straining to be at the throats of other poor fools as helpless as themselves. Why? Because the handful of men who control their destinies will, by lies and lies and still more lies, make it impossible for them to stay at home without appearing contemptible cravens.

A man and a woman, prosperous citizens. The man is carrying a large box of fruit and the woman a collecting basket and a small union jack.

CITIZEN	Fruit for the Fleet! It's Harvest Festival and I have collected one ton of apples and pears which I propose to despatch to the Navy at Dingwall.
LADY	Books for soldiers! Many of our recruits now are educated men and literature of a kind unsuitable for ordinary recruits would be welcomed by them.
CITIZEN	Plum Puddings for Bluejackets! Please send at least one plum pudding and I will forward them to the ships in the North Sea in time for Christmas.
LADY	Tobacco for the Tommies! We're raising funds to send 20,000 cigarettes to our Herts boys. SSS – smokes for sailors and soldiers.

A Territorial in training comes forward.

TERRY	One thing we haven't got is uniforms. There we are, training over at Panshanger and they say we have to wear our civvies until they get enough khaki for us

all. But we said no, we want regimentals. We're sick of people treating us Territorials as amateur soldiers, like we're just playing at it. Well, we should have kept our mouths shut because look what they've come up with for regulation issue. *(He shows white painter's overalls)*

(He sings to the tune of A Long Way to Tipperary:)

It's the wrong way to clothe a soldier
It's the wrong way, I know
It's the right way to clothe a painter
For the people tell me so.

EMILY   You can decorate my front room any time!

TERRY   Goodbye Territorials
Farewell RFA.
It's the wrong wrong way to clothe a soldier
But ain't my 'whites' gay?

Music of 'A Long Way to Tipperary' continues.

MERCURY   The government's Early Closing Bill has caused some controversy. Its supporters say restricting licensing hours will keep soldiers from temptation. Others express amazement that the authorities should be telling our men they can be trusted with the safety of the nation, yet cannot be trusted with an open public house.

Councillors gather for a meeting.

CHAIRMAN   Welcome to this meeting of the Rural District Council. When you see the thousands recruiting every day it only shows that the good old English spirit is there in time of need. As a captain in the Herts Yeomanry it is a great pang to me that a knee injury has prevented my following my duty to King and country *(Comments of 'too bad old chap')* God Save the King! *(Cheers)* Item one on the agenda, hunting.

CLLR   Puckeridge Hounds had a rattling good day amongst the cubs on Monday. Cubs were found in plenty. Three were killed at Hazel End Woods and two at Bailey Hills.

CHAIRMAN	But will the war put a stop to hunting?
CLLR	Not a bit of it Mr Chairman. The government has put in the word to hunts asking that the sport be continued, so as to help the farmers, encourage the breeding of horses and give young fellows a chance to learn to ride cross country. Hunting experience is the best experience for the Front! *(Applause)*

ANNIE and EFFIE, her daughter, come forward.

EFFIE	Effie Burnett Smith. Daughter of the more famous Annie. What is a woman to do? One of our generals supplied the answer. 'Tell the women and girls they can serve their country best by living quiet lives.' He obviously doesn't know much about girls.
MERCURY	The Hertford Voluntary Aid Detachment hospital with 24 beds has opened at Wallfields, commandeered from the nuns. There is a paid matron and volunteer nurses trained in first aid. One could almost wish one were a patient in the hands of such charming and attentive ladies!
ANNIE	There were plenty of activities to absorb women's energies and make them feel they were helping – at the Red Cross depots anxious and willing women spent hours rolling bandages. That sort of work did not appeal to me. Fortunately, Effie and I were able to work with the YMCA in France and off we went to Le Havre. I spoke in the huts every night, taking a message of gratitude and encouragement from the women at home. These young recruits were all Crusaders, eager and undismayed, because they were convinced of the righteousness of their cause. I did my best to write to their dear ones when I got home.
EFFIE	I didn't go home. There was a lot to do in France.

ANNIE and EFFIE hug and part.

Song: Sunshine of your smile.

MERCURY	A remarkable public meeting has been held at Essendon, called by Mr David Citroen of Essendon Place.

Essendon. People gather for a public meeting.

WOMAN 1	Have you heard? They were going to blow up Digswell Viaduct!
WOMAN 2	What?
WOMAN 1	The Germans!
MAN	They've blown up Digswell Viaduct?
WOMAN 2	But the Territorials were guarding it!
WOMAN 1	There was an enemy plot! The police searched that place, Libury Hall, and found all this dynamite in the piggery. So, they arrested a whole lot of the Germans and packed them off to Yorkshire.
WOMAN 2	Where d'you hear this?
WOMAN 1	My cousin in Hitchin. They put 'em on a train to Wakefield at Hitchin. She reckons there was two thousand people gathered at the station to boo them.

A smartly dressed man, DAVID CITROEN, takes the platform to address the meeting. He has a faint European accent.

CITROEN	Friends and neighbours. No-one is a more keen supporter of the British way of life than I.
MAN	Go home German!
CITROEN	I have lived in this country for twenty years...
MAN	Yer still a Hun.
CITROEN	Having been born in Amsterdam. My dear wife is British, I am a naturalised British citizen and was, until my retirement, chairman of a British company, the Minerva Motor Manufacturing Company Ltd.
MAN	Yer a spy and you know it.

CITROEN	I have lived at Essendon Place for twelve years, you all know me, you see me at church, you come to our annual garden party and now, when our German enemy is threatening my homeland as it threatens yours, you turn on me and accuse me of being a traitor. I've called this public meeting to clear my name and if anyone continues to slander me after this they are dastardly cowards.
WOMAN 1	What about all that concrete then?
CITROEN	What?
WOMAN 1	All that concrete you been putting in your garden. For gun placements.
CITROEN	I've been having my terrace relaid.
WOMAN 2	You been interrogated by the army.
CITROEN	I invited Military Intelligence to inspect my house and estate and satisfy themselves that there was nothing to indicate suspicious enemy activity.
WOMAN 1	Well my neighbour's daughter in law said it was common knowledge that you were fortifying your house for the Kaiser to use as his headquarters for when the Germans invade…
MAN	And you were putting in bomb proof windows.
WOMAN 2	And gun batteries on the lawn.
CITROEN	And you believed this?
MAN	… Well, no.
CITROEN	You think I have pulled the wool over Military Intelligence's eyes?
MAN	'Course not.
WOMAN 1	I said, never that Mr Citroen. He's such a nice man.
MAN	Very generous to Essendon.

WOMAN 1   So course we knew it was a nonsense.

CITROEN   Good. Well. I hope we will hear no more of it.

They all start up with 'For he's a jolly good fellow'.

CITROEN   Oh, come now. *(Pompously pleased)*

CLAUD SWEENEY, in the trenches. There is a sound of explosions. He throws himself down.

MERCURY   So the 1st battalion have had their baptism of fire…

ELIZABETH comes on, reading a letter from Claud.

MERCURY   … and come through, as we knew they would.

SWEENEY sits up and looks around.

SWEENEY   It is hell on earth here.

He stands up and dusts himself off.

SWEENEY   That was it, I suppose. Our first real action at the front, fourteenth of November 1914, somewhere near Wipers. They say we got off lightly. Fifteen dead, 35 wounded. Two buried alive in the trenches. I can't remember anything about that day. Not a thing. I remember the afterwards. The thirst. We were two days without water. The officers shared their bottles with the men. *(He is astonished)* They really did Mum. And the joke is, the rain. It doesn't stop raining, day or night. Two things that never stop. The rain and the guns.

Music – 'Silent Night'.

MERCURY   Christmas comes despite the war! Chocolates, desserts, Stilton, Cheddar and Gorgonzola. Tea in fancy canisters. The ideal present. Christmas presents for smokers. C&J Law of St Andrew Street are making giant cigarettes for the season. All cigarettes guaranteed free from sand and dust.

In the trenches.

SWEENEY Christmas. I think. You know Albert Hawkes, the Herts Lark? One of us Ware boys. He's been keeping up the seasonal mood with his singing.

A few lines of 'Silent Night' are heard.

SWEENEY There's rumours it's a truce but nobody seems to know for sure... The 1st Herts have got a new nickname now. We kept up such a good pace on the march a couple of days ago that some Guards officer said we weren't Terriers, more like Greyhounds. Guards! They're normally so stuck up, being professionals not mere volunteers. We're here alongside Indian soldiers in turbans now. I'm seeing the world. But reminded of home. You know Huggins Furniture on the high street? Percy Huggins is here.

HUGGINS, joins him, crumpled and yawning. Like SWEENEY, he is very young.

SWEENEY Alright Huggins?

HUGGINS Would be if I could get some sleep.

SWEENEY Ask your dad to send over a couple of feather beds.

HUGGINS The officers would bag them.

SWEENEY Look at you Huggins. Thought you Grammar boys were supposed to look smart.

HUGGINS Put a sock in it Sweeney. And keep low. There's a sniper about.

SWEENEY Heard they're swapping rum rations for schnapps up the line.

HUGGINS I'm not getting friendly with Fritz.

Singing is heard – Stille Nacht.

HUGGINS Is that Hawkes?

SWEENEY Not unless he's turned German.

HUGGINS Sounds like him.

He shifts his position, slightly raising his head. There is a shot, he falls, killed by the sniper.

Stille Nacht continues.

MERCURY	The Great Resolution for the New Year – I will be a MAN and enlist today. Mr Hensby, Headmaster of Buckland School, Buntingford, has written to the Mercury to deny that he has evaded military service despite being a member of the Territorials. On Wednesday night there was rough music in the town, outside his house.

Discordant music, which fades away to a droning noise, as of engines in the sky. ANNIE SWAN comes on and looks upwards.

ANNIE	In 1915 the Zeppelins arrived. They were a curiosity to begin with. We didn't realise how much they would come to dominate our lives. The war was grinding on, but not much was different yet at home.

WILLIAM GRAVESON steps forward. COUNCILLORS are gathered for a meeting.

GRAVESON	William Graveson, owner of the haberdashery shop with my brother Alfred, justice of the peace, member of the county council's education committee, former mayor of Hertford and sometimes – it seems – one man opposition on Hertford Town Council! I would like to raise the matter once again of facilities for the troops in the town…
CLLR	No baths on the rates Mr Graveson!
GRAVESON	Admittedly it would be a cost to the ratepayer to install public baths, but many residents would also benefit *(other councillors jeer and hold their noses)* and you cannot deny that the town has gained financially from so many troops…
CLLR	The corporation is not here to provide domestic conveniences…
GRAVESON	Public health…
CLLR	Socialistic nonsense sir.

GRAVESON   I see I shall always be outvoted by an element on this council distinctly lacking in vision and enterprise!

CLLR   If it's enterprise you want, why doesn't someone set up some tubs and hot water in Market Square and charge the men thruppence a wash. Earn a fortune!

Laughter from the councillors. GRAVESON frustrated.

Music – Cello playing 'A Long Way to Tipperary' in minor.

CORPORAL BURT comes on, filthy, caked in mud.

BURT   Corporal Alfred Burt. 1st Herts. It's still raining. The trenches are running rivers. We're constantly on the move, slogging from place to place but our feet are caked with mud, slipping backwards with every step we take. It feels like the whole world is in ruins. One day we came through a French village where everything was entirely shattered. The church steeple had fallen, with the point embedded in the earth. Anyway, today we're in this dugout, not knowing what's coming next, gas, fizz bangs, pipsqueaks. Then a German rumjar bomb comes bouncing in. I wasn't even thinking.

A large mortar bomb lands at his feet. Swiftly, he puts his foot on the fuse, pulls it out and throws it over the parapet.

He stands rather stunned, looking at the defused bomb. Then others come on, stare, slap him on the back – 'Alf, you did it!' 'You saved us!' etc.

MERCURY   Hertford's hero! Corporal Alfred Burt, son of Mr and Mrs Thomas Burt of 19 Nelson Street, has been awarded the Victoria Cross, for conspicuous bravery at Cuinchy, on the 27th September 1915.

BURT   It wasn't really bravery. I just did it.

MERCURY   With his presence of mind and great pluck, Corporal Burt's cool act saved the lives of maybe twenty of his comrades.

'Tipperary' again, played jauntily.

Night time. POLICEMAN comes on.

| POLICE | The thirteenth of October 1915. I was doing my rounds on Bull Plain. I stopped to have a word with two gentlemen outside Lombard House, whom I knew to be Mr Gregory, the organist at All Saints, and Mr Jevons the Borough Engineer. |

There is a noise in the sky. They look up.

JEVONS	Ha! It's one of those chaps.
GREGORY	Heading for London I should think.
JEVONS	Sounds close - we might get a good look at it. Fascinating machines.
GREGORY	There speaks an engineer Jevons! They're not fascinating, they're filthy things. Done horrible damage on the east coast.
JEVONS	But German engineering... Still. We'll get the better of them soon.

ANNIE comes on.

ANNIE	The Zeppelin – our Zeppelin – an L16 commanded by Werner Peterson, was one of five which had arrived on the east coast.
POLICE	Gentlemen. Perhaps you should go inside.
JEVONS	Don't you want to see a Zeppelin constable?
POLICE	I'd rather stay safe sir. You should go back into the club.
JEVONS	Oh it's not interested in us.
ANNIE	But the Zeppelins were detected by searchlights and had to scatter and fly higher. They lost their bearings. They looked for towns, lit by gaslight, and stretches of water reflecting the moonlight. Peterson and his crew saw what they were looking for - a curving ribbon of water. L16 moved along the river until lights came into view below.

The noise of the Zeppelin gets closer and louder. JEVONS and GREGORY move out into the street peering upwards. The POLICEMAN hangs back.

ANNIE Peterson dropped his 48 bombs, and headed for home, reporting a successful raid on industrial and railway targets in east London.

There is a tremendous explosion. A bomb makes a direct hit on Bull Plain.

The POLICEMAN crawls out on his hands and knees, stands up shakily. ANNIE is nowhere to be seen.

POLICE I looked for Mr Gregory and Mr Jevons... I... I couldn't really find them. I mean... There was hardly anything left of them. I have to report that nine people were killed in less than two minutes. The first bombs dropped on the Folly. Then Bull Plain. Then Old Cross was hit and North Road. A high explosive bomb fell outside the gates of Hertford County hospital and two workmen across the road died. As well as Mr Gregory and Mr Jevons, the dead were Acting Bombardier Arthur Cox, Arthur Hart, Ernie Jolly, Charles Spicer, Charles Waller. And George Game. Aged three. Hit by shrapnel which came through the wall of his bedroom.

ANNIE appears, in shock.

ANNIE I'm alive. Eight bombs fell on our house in North Road. Three on the house and five on the garden and only the poor cats were killed sleeping in their chairs when the kitchen was blown up. *(She laughs, on the edge of breaking down).* It's all Effie's fault. Only the day before, when she arrived home on leave from France, she said...

EFFIE I'd love to see a Zeppelin raid! At our base there's no such luck.

The noise of a Zeppelin engine getting nearer.

ANNIE That evening, Jim was out on his rounds. We had finished dinner, then the town was plunged into darkness when the first bomb destroyed the gasworks. We rushed outside to see what was happening.

EFFIE	Our cook and our maid came running out of the kitchen. That saved their lives.

They stand looking upwards.

ANNIE	A few minutes. An interlude in which that ship passed slowly over our town, dropping death. And visiting us last.

They clutch each other, terrified, as the bombs fall.

EFFIE	Is this it Mum? Will this be the one?

They brace themselves, but after the bombs the Zeppelin passes over. All goes quiet.

EFFIE	Nearly all our stuff was ruined. But our after-dinner tea was still on its tray, not a drop spilled. You never know, what will be destroyed and what will be saved.

ANNIE	We were saved. As Jim said when he found us, that is what matters. Poor Jim. Some kind soul had rushed to tell him his house and everyone in it had been obliterated.

EFFIE	Next morning North Road was packed with people. Word had got around that Hertford had been wiped off the map so people had come up from London to see. Of course there was no mention of the raid in any newspaper. All that was published was 'Air attack on London successfully driven off'.

ANNIE	We couldn't stay in the house. With no front door and no windows, the wind whistled straight through it and not just the wind… Excuse me!

She stops a well-dressed man who is going past carrying items of china.

ANNIE	That is my dinner service I believe!

MAN	Just a little souvenir of the great air raid! This could be valuable.

ANNIE	It is valuable to me! I eat off it.

MAN	Honestly, some people.
MERCURY	Latest acquisitions by Hertford Museum. Specimens of Army biscuits made by Messrs Gilbertson and Page, Hertford. A bomb that didn't go off at Ypres. Six fine cases of fish. Two small cases of birds.

ELIZABETH gets a letter. EMILY tries to comfort her.

EMILY	John! Oh no I don't believe it. Oh Elizabeth I'm so sorry.
ELIZABETH	He shouldn't even have been there…
EMILY	Elizabeth…
ELIZABETH	A man of 45 lying about his age. So ridiculous. He had to enlist in the Bedfordshires because everyone in the Territorials knew how old he was.
EMILY	He wanted to do his duty, like his son.
ELIZABETH	Men are so stupid… I knew this would happen. John was no soldier. And he'd only been in France a month… And what about Claud?
EMILY	Claud will be alright. He can run faster than a bullet. Remember when he was diving into the Lea off the toll bridge?
ELIZABETH	Such a show off… Oh John… I'll never see him again. Emily my own husband, I'm never going to see him again…

Song: to the tune of 'Good King Wenceslas'.

Good Lord Derby looked around
And his eyes were shooting
Angry glances when he found
Very slow recruiting.
Wake up Englishmen he cried
Else you'll drive me barmy
Do your duty one and all
Come and join the Army!

MERCURY   1916. A new year. Proposals are in place for
                compulsory national military service, to come into
                force on the first of March this year. One thing is
                certain. Every woman who has a son or husband in
                the firing line will prove a conscriptionist at heart.
                She will ask why her man should be taken and
                others left. Those fighting at the front are also
                making their views known. Here is a letter to the
                editor from Driver C Wellman at the Front. 'Dear
                sir. The lads have got me to write to you at the
                Mercury and send a message to all you young men
                of Hertford. We can do with all you young chaps.
                You know that it is not right for some of us to get
                killed and for some of you to stay at home and enjoy
                yourselves walking up and down Fore Street all day
                and night. We're having a splendid time out here
                and you can do the same. Yours sincerely.'

WILLIAM GRAVESON sits as magistrate.

GRAVESON   Hertfordshire's crime figures have gone up in recent
                months. This is largely due to the number of
                prosecutions for breaching lighting orders.
                Madam…

EMILY   It was a tiny candle sir.

GRAVESON   It was a light.

EMILY   A Zepp isn't going to see a little candle from six
                thousand feet up.

GRAVESON   On the contrary, when the countryside is in
                darkness, a little candle, a cigarette even, is all they
                need to tell them there is habitation down there. Two
                shillings fine.

MAJOR KINMAN comes before the bench, somewhat embarrassed.

GRAVESON   Major Kinman!

KINMAN   I know William, I know…

GRAVESON   Lights showing at Bayley Hall. Was it one of the
                servants?

KINMAN	Actually one of the dogs was barking to be let out and Mrs Kinman… Anyway, I'd better pay up.
GRAVESON	I'm afraid so Major. Two shillings fine.
MERCURY	From the classifieds. Twelfth of February 1916. House. Suitable for school, at Malvern, Worcestershire. Healthy position, lovely country. Rent moderate. No zeppelins.
	Mourning orders by post. Ladies' costumes dyed black 5 shillings. Blouses dyed black one shilling. We guarantee a good, fast black. J Smith and Co, Cleaners and Dyers, Bradford.

CORPORAL BURT, weary, in muddy uniform, carrying a kitbag, comes on. The Town Hall CLERK grabs him.

CLERK	Corporal Burt! It's an honour, an honour! Come with me…
BURT	What…?
CLERK	We got a telephone call from the Stationmaster at Broxbourne station. He said he thought he recognised this chap and it's you, Corporal Burt! Back from the trenches in person. I told the Mayor – don't worry. I'm going to nab him and bring him to the council chamber!
BURT	But I'm just going to my Mother's.
CLERK	Come on sir, mustn't keep the Mayor waiting.

The MAYOR strides forward, hastily putting on his chain, and shakes his hand.

MAYOR	Corporal Burt, VC. *(applause)* On behalf of the Corporation and inhabitants of Hertford, your native town, I welcome you sincerely here tonight. Later on we shall give you a more formal welcome, but we thought it would be a nice thing if we could get you here to our council meeting at once and show you we have not forgotten you.
BURT	Thank you sir, I…

MAYOR   Kindly convey to your parents the fact that we are going to send a letter of congratulation to them and also to the Commanding Officer of your regiment. *(Hear hear)* And as this is a unique occasion, I move that it be entered in the minutes so that future generations might see what this little town is capable of.

Applause all round.

BURT   Thank you sir. Mr Mayor… *(awkward pause)* Can I go now? *(He backs out)*

MAYOR   Ah. What modesty. We need more like him.

With honks of a motor horn, NOEL PEMBERTON-BILLING (P-B) zooms on.

MERCURY   The East Herts by-election. Surprise development.

PEMBERTON-BILLING goes round shaking as many people as possible by the hand.

P-B   Good day, good day! I hope I may count on your vote.

MERCURY   In the forthcoming by-election, there are to be two candidates. While the Conservatives and Unionists and the Liberals have agreed not to field opposing candidates in by-elections, as they are now coalition partners in our national wartime government, there is nothing to stop independent candidates putting themselves forward. Mr Noel Pemberton-Billing has already contested the Mile End by-election, unsuccessfully. Now he is to try his hand in East Herts, standing against the Unionist candidate and well-known Hertfordshire man, Mr Brodie Henderson.

P-B   Vote for Pemberton-Billing! The Air Candidate!

SUPPORTER   No more Zepps!

P-B   Exactly. What do you people of East Herts need? Safe skies! I'm not a politician, I'm a businessman and a flyer. You are voting at a crucial time – a time when politics should be sacrificed for the one great

	object – the protection of the country from hostile aircraft!
HECKLER	Who are you anyway? What's your party? Isn't this just your little hobby horse, supported by the Daily Mail for the sole purpose of harassing the national government?
P-B	I know what I stand for. I stand for British supremacy in the air!
SUPPORTER	Vote for Pemberton-Billing and say goodbye to Zeppelin raids!
P-B	I don't actually claim <u>that</u>…
HECKLER	Here you are, swooping down from the sky like some vulture to East Herts only because this part of the world has suffered so badly from the Zeppelins.
P-B	You have suffered, and whose fault is that?
HECKLER	The Germans.
P-B	And who has failed to protect you? Your own government.
HECKLER	The government is building the finest aircraft that the world has ever seen.
P-B	What do you know about aircraft? I built my first biplane in 1904. I designed my flying boat in 1911. Vote for me and I will ensure we achieve the air supremacy we deserve!

Cheers and boos etc. The HECKLER and the SUPPORTER of P-B argue.

SUPPORTER	He'll show those stuffed shirts in the House of Commons.
HECKLER	But this is no time for a man to be paddling his own canoe in Parliament. We need a united front.
SUPPORTER	We've got a unity government and a fat lot of good it's done us so far in France.

HECKLER   He's a puppet of the Daily Mail. They make him out to be the little man fighting against the Coalition machine.

SUPPORTER   Maybe we don't all want to be cogs in the machine. This isn't Germany. A man here has a right to stand up and say what he wants.

HECKLER   But we're at war! An attack on the government is a victory for the Germans. We all know there's spies everywhere. They must be rubbing their hands with glee at Pemberton-Billing's antics. The downfall of the government would be worth more to them than a victory at Verdun.

Song: 'Onward Christian Soldiers'.

MERCURY   If YOU cannot wear khaki – do the next best thing. Wear one of our stylish city suits and keep up Old England's reputation for well-dressed men. Drury Brothers, Maidenhead Street, Hertford.

MAJOR KINMAN enters, in uniform, sets up his table for the first session of the Hertford Military Service Tribunal. He addresses the room sternly.

KINMAN   Major Kinman. I am the army representative on the Hertford Military Service Tribunal and today I will be chairing it. A few ground rules. We are prepared to let every man have his say but leave your soapbox at home. Under the Military Service Act of 27th January 1916 you are already all soldiers. All men between the ages of 19 and 41 who are single, or a widower without dependent children, are deemed to have enlisted for general service. If you want exemption, absolute, conditional or temporary, for yourself or your employee, you'd better have a good reason. We will not be a soft touch but we will judge each case on its merits. Our hope is that the men of Hertfordshire will see their duty. Right. Let's get started. First?

BAKER   I've got a bakery on the High Street, in Ware. They've called up my chap Joe.

KINMAN   And?

BAKER	I can't do without Joe.
KINMAN	How many other employees do you have?
BAKER	Four. But Joe's the strongest. He's the boy for lifting a sack of flour.
KINMAN	Then he will make an excellent soldier. Do you want to go Joe?
JOE	*(From off)* I do sir.
BAKER	Shut up Joe. I'll tell your mother.
KINMAN	Exemption refused. Next.
GRAVES	I'm cellarman at the Salisbury Tap. Reckon there's been a mistake sir. I ain't fit to be a soldier.
KINMAN	Really? Why is that?
GRAVES	Well. I only got one eye sir. See?

He pops his glass eye into his hand and holds it up.

KINMAN	Thank you. Exemption granted.
DIXON	Arthur Dixon.
KINMAN	Ah. You're the objector.
DIXON	The law allows for conscientious objection to military service.
KINMAN	You are a Quaker?
DIXON	I attend the Friends' meetings.
KINMAN	Many of your fellows have joined the Friends' ambulance service. Mr William Graveson's son Arthur is with them at the front. I'm sure they would welcome you. If you are not a coward. Young Graveson has already been on one hospital ship torpedoed in the Channel.

DIXON   The ambulance service is part of the military campaign. The Society of Friends believes that to force any man against his conscience to be a party to the killing of another man is oppression of the worst kind.

KINMAN   You would be helping your fellow men, not killing them.

DIXON   I would be part of the military machine sir and I cannot be. To serve the war, in my view, means entrenching more deeply that militarism from which we all desire the world to be freed.

KINMAN   Mr Dixon I do not intend to argue with you. I will refer your case to the Central Tribunal to get some kind of ruling which will guide us in future appeals from objectors. No doubt there will be many.

MERCURY   What may prove to be a social revolution is approaching, as a direct consequence of the war. The government wishes to mobilise a force of 400,000 ... women, to replace the agricultural workers going to the front. Farmers must pay them the same wages as the men...

FARMER   What!

MERCURY   Men must not fear that they will go off to war and have their wages undercut by female replacements.

FARMER   But women! Why should we pay them anything at all?

MERCURY   Equal wages should be paid for equal work.

FARMER   It's not fair. They should do it for their country.

MERCURY   Nothing could be more unfair than to underpay women on the grounds that they should make a patriotic sacrifice. Male workers have not been asked to do that. On the contrary, they have been earning war bonuses. For their part, women must show that they are up to the task of equal work.

FARMER	The world's gone mad.
MERCURY	Lady Salisbury is holding a meeting at the Old Palace, Hatfield…
LADY S	This country is heavily reliant on imports from the dominions for its daily bread. But the shipments are not getting through and the nation must feed itself, while our young men are leaving the land and joining the forces. So the country is looking to its womenfolk. If women are prepared to take on agricultural work, they would be winning the war as much as if they went out to fight. There is a great deal they can do, as Miss Puller will explain.
LOUISA	Thank you Lady Salisbury. Let me tell you, ladies, about the joys of mangolds and muck. I've tried it for myself – I've been out there pulling mangolds, planting cabbages and, yes, spreading manure. Work on the land is in the open and very healthy. So come on girls. Let's have work squads from every town and village in East Herts and show the doubters what women can do!
LADY S	*(Aside)* Well said Louisa.
LOUISA	We can't vote but we can work eh?
LADY S	It's a good thing women can't vote because too many are being taken in by this Pemberton-Billing.
LOUISA	The dashing flyer? I wouldn't vote for him though.
LADY S	No?
LOUISA	All talk.
MERCURY	Surprise result of East Herts election! The Air Candidate wins! Sweeps to victory after hurricane campaign!

Cheers from supporters. PEMBERTON-BILLING enjoys the acclaim.

P-B	Thank you thank you. Your vote has changed the course of this nation. The Daily Mail says, 'The vote

	is a bomb dropped on Downing Street as a violent hint to the muddlers and the drifters'.
HECKLER	It's the Hustler from East Herts.
P-B	All I care about is action. We need air attacks on Germany in retaliation for the Zeppelin raids. Public opinion knows I'm right. *(applause, hear hear etc)* But this is not just about air raids. This is about our brave pilots and the government that has betrayed them! Yes! Why are we not winning the battle in the air? Because gallant officers in the Royal Flying Corps are being murdered!
HECKLER	That's a filthy accusation.
P-B	They have been given aeroplanes so poorly designed and built that to send a man up in one is an act of murder! And I will prove that! *(boos, cheers)*. I have compiled a list of accidents and known faults in aircraft which I am putting to the Ministry. I am calling for the creation of a new Imperial Air Service, and I ask the voters of East Hertfordshire to sign my air covenant today! Also, my book is now on sale – 'Air War and How to Wage It'. I have copies…

He is surrounded by crowd, buying books, signing the air covenant, asking him to sign their book etc.

Music: 'We plough the fields and scatter'.

LOUISA PULLER and JENNY MASON, in the fields.

LOUISA	I'm a farm labourer now! See my green armlet. Here we are, potato dropping and thistle spudding. This is Jenny Mason, in charge of a team from the village. You've got a good squad, haven't you Jenny?
JENNY	I have, though they've been moaning today. We got a list through of the recognised costume for the woman worker. *(Looks at list)* Coat 9 shillings and 11d; knickerbockers in soft drill 2 shillings.
LOUISA	Don't they like the knickerbockers?
JENNY	They don't like the two shillings.

LOUISA	They'll have to do their best. We're having fun aren't we Jenny?
JENNY	We are Miss Puller and at the start I didn't think I'd be saying that. I volunteered because I wanted to do my bit, with Ernest in France. But tell the truth, farm work is a different kind of thing from women's work, which is usually clearing other people's mess. We're helping to grow something, not mending a muddle which will be just as muddled tomorrow.
LOUISA	And you're leading a whole squad of workers too. What does Ernest say to that?
JENNY	Well, I haven't mentioned it in my letters yet.

The FARMER arrives to watch them working.

LOUISA	The women are doing well I think.
FARMER	Alright at potato dropping. Slow at hoeing. I shall have to put up with that.
LOUISA	*(Undaunted)* We had a competition last week for hoeing and root singling. Workers from Standon, Puckeridge, Braughing, High Cross and the Hadhams. A great many turnips were slaughtered I'm afraid but it was in a good cause. We beat Buntingford fair and square. The spectators were rather impressed.
FARMER	You're telling me. All those girls in breeches!
LOUISA	And Mrs Abel Smith has set up a model dairy over at Stapleford where girls can learn milking. There is a hostel for the girls and they receive six weeks training until they are qualified for dairy work.
FARMER	The farmers will never have them.
JENNY	They will have to, won't they sir, when their dairymen are called up.
LOUISA	We've been asked to pick flowers too.
FARMER	That's more like it.

JENNY   Poisonous ones.

LOUISA   Yes. Apparently all sorts of plants are used in medicines, and up till now this kind of herb culture has been monopolised by the Germans. Now we need to do it ourselves. So at the moment, we're to collect foxgloves and white bryony. It makes you look at the hedgerows in a different way.

MERCURY   April 1916. We must press on. Already, conscription is being extended, calling up the boy of 18, the married man, and the time-expired man who has already seen the hell of the trenches. The new act, with all its home breaking and heart wrenching, will bring the war to all. Every one among us, man, woman and even child, must realise that citizenship in a free state is not a shareholding in a profit making concern, in which individual liability is strictly limited. It is more like a joint stock concern. We are all in this.

Music: Elgar

W E JOHNS   I spent the first years of the war at Salonika. Boiling in the summer, freezing in the winter. I survived the shells and the snipers but the mosquitoes nearly got me. I was shipped out with malaria. I put in for a transfer to the Royal Flying Corps. It seemed to me there was no point dying standing up in squalor if you could do so sitting down in clean air. I took to flying pretty quickly. Had a few crashes but still loved it. One morning a pal and I at the base in Norfolk were both down for early flying, sharing the same machine. He volunteered to take her up first and I watched out of the window while I shaved. At about 2000 feet the aircraft started to turn. The port wing of the plane went up like a sunshade blown inside out. The aircraft went into a dive and I saw my friend climb out and jump. He had no parachute of course, no one did. He had a horror of burning to death.

ANNIE   In the summer of 1916 I went to France again to work with the YMCA. It was very different from 1914. The glow and glory was dimmed, the spirit of the Crusaders only existing in patches. These were conscripted men, full of doubts and questioning, talking of 'Fritz', not as an enemy, but a comrade in misfortune. By July 1916, the Somme offensive, 420 thousand men were dead, more than twice the number of the entire army in 1914. The old British army was gone and the military were often struggling to know what to do with conscripts, whom they had never had before. At home they struggled even more. What do you do with conscripts who refuse to fight?

The Tribunal. DIXON, conscientious objector, is back before KINMAN.

KINMAN Mr Dixon. You're here again. What exactly is it that you want?

DIXON Non-combatant status.

KINMAN Mr Dixon. You have a right to apply for non-com status. But if you had been at the county appeal tribunal with me last week and seen the long haired, lantern jawed, vegetarian types so typical of Letchworth who paraded before us for non-combatant status, you would think again! I don't want to see any man of this town put amongst those people and I want, if possible, to get you to withdraw your application.

DIXON I cannot do that.

KINMAN You can. A number of your fellow Quakers have asked to be taken out of non-combatant status and have simply opted to work on the land, which is acceptable.

DIXON I will not fight. So a non-combatant is what I am. I know the consequences.

The CLERK steps in, holding a Bible.

CLERK Mr Chairman, if I may. Mr Dixon, did not God himself give the Israelites victory in battle?

DIXON But in the Sermon on the Mount, Christ says blessed are the peacemakers.

CLERK	Peacemakers, not pacifists.
KINMAN	The issue is really Mr Dixon whether you are prepared to work on the land…
CLERK	Yet does it not say in Deuteronomy, 'Shall your brethren go to war and shall ye sit here…?'
KINMAN	Gentlemen please! Just get yourself off to a farm Mr Dixon. If the women can do it, you can and no-one has to spend any more time filleting the Bible for ammunition for their cause.

They move away and KINMAN reflects despairingly.

KINMAN	And the conchies are not the worst of them. 'You can't have my ploughman. I know Lord Salisbury.' 'I can't spare my coachman. I have six hunters and four carriage horses in stables!'
SANSOM	Sir? I am a watercress grower sir. My two brothers are both gone to the army. If I'm called up the business will be lost entirely and I got a letter here from my brothers to say that they've invested five hundred pounds in the business and don't want to see it ruined.
KINMAN	Six months exemption.

Protests from others – 'That's not fair', 'Why him not me?' 'I deserve exemption more' etc

KINMAN	Next? Mr Russell Johns? Ah – Johns Minor. How are you my boy?

RUSSELL JOHNS, brother of BILL JOHNS, looking embarrassed to be before his old headmaster.

RUSSELL	All right sir.
KINMAN	How's that brother of yours? Still alive?
RUSSELL	Still alive sir.
KINMAN	The school door still bears the burn marks from where you and he tried to set it alight with a

	firework. Your brother's idea I expect. Hm. You want exemption?
RUSSELL	It's just that... mother only has me, with father dead and Bill gone.
KINMAN	You had wanted to go to university to study chemistry, hadn't you? But you stayed for your mother.
RUSSELL	It seemed the thing was to carry on my father's photography business.
KINMAN	You're going to have to go Johns.
RUSSELL	I know.
KINMAN	Your mother will get your allowance. I can give you two months exemption to arrange your affairs. Will that help?
RUSSELL	Thank you sir.

The Ware Stink. EMILY and ELIZABETH enter, with hankies over their noses.

EMILY	Have you heard from Claud?
ELIZABETH	I get letters. They don't say nothing of course.
EMILY	That doesn't matter as long as you keep getting them. Pwooah. What IS this stink?
ELIZABETH	It's those barges of grain. They've gone off.
EMILY	What barges?
ELIZABETH	I don't know. Mr Ward has brought them up the river and they're sitting there, ponging to high heaven.
EMILY	In this hot weather!
WARD	This is salvage grain, madam. Heroically rescued from a ship torpedoed in the North Sea. Nothing wrong with it.

EMILY	'Cept it's rotten.
ELIZABETH	It's making us all feel sick.
WARD	I can assure you it will be perfectly alright for animal feed. A bargain at only two pounds a ton.
ELIZABETH	Even the rats won't touch it! Phwoo.
EMILY	Someone should report you to the police Mr Ward. Making people's lives a misery in this town.
WARD	I'm doing my duty. It's a pity other people aren't so patriotic! For the sake of the nation I'm not letting good grain go to waste.

Music. 'For those in peril on the sea'.

MERCURY	Tragic loss of the HMS Hampshire. Kitchener drowned. Leading Seaman Charles Rogerson from Bengeo is last man to see Kitchener alive.

A sailor, CHARLES ROGERSON, comes on, bedraggled and exhausted.

ROGERSON	We were taking Lord Kitchener to Russia. I believe we struck a mine – anyway, the ship sank in quarter of an hour. Some of us managed to get on to rafts. As I jumped I saw Lord Kitchener talking to his officers. The ship went down so soon after that I am sure Lord Kitchener went down with her, despite people saying it can't be true. It was hell on the rafts. Men were killed from being buffeted by the sea and others died from the fearful cold. An almost overpowering desire to go to sleep comes over you and we thumped each other on the back, because if you went to sleep you never woke up again. I believe only 12 of us survived.

Silence.

Music: 'All things bright and beautiful'.

Cheery infant school TEACHER and some children come on, clutching sheets of newspaper and waving Belgian flags.

TEACHER	Welcome everybody to Braughing Elementary School's fundraising afternoon in aid of the Belgian

refugees. The children have done marvellous work for the war effort. We have had many nature walks which have been most productive. The children have collected acorns for animal feed, and nutshells and fruit stones to make charcoal for gas masks! We will now have a demonstration of children's paper cutting on the theme of His Majesty's Fleet.

Children cut out shapes and stick them on a board or hold them up. Music plays.

TEACHER	Very good Henry and what is this?
HENRY	This is a warship Miss and this 'ere is a submarine. *(Applause)*
TEACHER	And our cutouts can all be purchased.
HENRY	Thruppence, thruppence, who'll give me thruppence, going once, twice…
TEACHER	Thank you Henry. I'm delighted to say the Braughing children between them have raised six pounds for the poor refugees.

The children sing a ragged version of 'Keep the Home Fires Burning' and salute in military style.

MERCURY	The fourth of August 1916. The British Empire is being tested as with fire, and pure gold will emerge from the furnace. Because the outstanding gain has been the discovery that the British people still possess a soul. Before the war, luxury was rampant, ease was idolised, self-indulgence and money-worship had passed into a cult. But when war came, thousands volunteered, as every true Briton felt instinctively that what was involved was the cause of liberty, humanity and civilisation.

FREDA, a well-dressed lady, comes on, holding a trowel and a tray of seedlings. Followed by her FRIEND.

FREDA	The mayor has called for volunteers to keep the grounds of Hertford Castle looking nice. I came straight away with a tray of begonias.

FRIEND	You're wasting your time Freda.
FREDA	I disagree. The Castle grounds give pleasure to anyone, at no charge, and there is precious little pleasure in our lives any more.
FRIEND	I'm not saying the grounds should be neglected but nothing beyond what is absolutely necessary should be done to them while the war lasts. Your effort would be better spent maintaining the garden of a serving soldier or turning over your rose bed to fruit and veg.
FREDA	I think you're very severe.
FRIEND	I'm practical Freda. We could all do with being more practical.
MERCURY	Buntingford schoolchildren have to date collected 2000 eggs for wounded soldiers. Central Control Board Liquor Restrictions come into force on Monday. Intoxicating liquors can only be sold within the hours of 12 noon to 2.30pm and six to 8 pm. Spirits may only be sold 12 noon to 2.30pm, no evening sales, no Saturday sales.

Groans all round.

LOUISA PULLER, JENNY MASON and the FARMER, out in the fields, LOUISA and JENNY working hard.

JENNY	It's war – on weeds! *(She and LOUISA laugh. The FARMER sighs gloomily)*
LOUISA	What's up?
FARMER	Harvest'll be a disaster at this rate.
LOUISA	Not at all. The weather's been lovely.
FARMER	I haven't got the workers Miss Puller!
LOUISA	I heard the county council had negotiated 500 soldiers for harvest.

FARMER	We've been promised labour before and it's not been forthcoming.
LOUISA	We've got London women here now. Art students from the Slade, women up from Stoke Newington who've never seen a turnip in the raw before but they certainly know how to work. The boys from the grammar school are going to pitch in with the harvest. The children are helping.
JENNY	Sort of.
FARMER	Hm.
LOUISA	There's the COs.
FARMER	Bunch of lily-livered shirkers!
LOUISA	Surely the haymaking has gone well?
FARMER	'Spose the girls have done alright. They're slow but they're thorough.
LOUISA	It's all in the organisation.
FARMER	I never thought they'd cope with the long hours to be honest but they were here till nine o'clock last night.
LOUISA	Jenny?
JENNY	Miss Puller?
LOUISA	What time were you up this morning?
JENNY	Five. As usual.
LOUISA	Why?
JENNY	Well, to get some washing done and hung out and the kids' breakfasts and dinner.
LOUISA	And how much housework will you do after you go home this evening?
JENNY	Another couple of hours I should think! *(She laughs)*

LOUISA turns to the FARMER and smiles.

Music: Cello, pastoral

MERCURY   Thanks to daylight saving, the worker has the opportunity for a quiet country ramble after the day's toil is over and before the searchlights show it is time to be abed. As the summer spins itself towards its close, there is something strangely soothing in the landscape at the fall of an evening. The lines of the poet Grey spring to mind – 'Now fades the glimmering landscape to the view, And all the world a solemn stillness holds'…

People look up, gasp and point. 'It's coming over, it's… Get inside, take cover…' 'No it's going over that way…' 'Look, look, they're flying… They're getting him…'

W E JOHNS   21 year old Lieutenant Leefe Robinson was flying a converted BE2c night fighter. On the third of September 1916, he had been patrolling for about three hours when at 2am he saw a Zeppelin north of London, picked out by the searchlights. He reported afterwards: 'I saw shells bursting and night tracers around it but the anti-aircraft aim was too high or too low. I got behind it, very close – 500 feet or less – and concentrated one drum from my machine gun on the underneath rear. In a few seconds the whole rear was blazing.' To the huge excitement of Hertfordshire, the stricken airship fell to earth in a field at Cuffley.

Cuffley. The morning after. Two Scouts are out, searching the wreckage and re-enacting the fight. One holds up something as the airship and drops stones as bombs. The other flies a twig for a bi-plane around it, making aeroplane noises.

SCOUT 1   *(With plane)* Wheee…

SCOUT 2   *(With Zepp)* Boom… Boom… I've bombed Essendon… now I'm going to blow up Enfield… boom!

SCOUT 1   Die Huns… takataka

SCOUT 2   Urgh… *(Starts to drop)*

SCOUT 1	No it didn't drop straight away. It sort of hung there all wriggling and burning.
SCOUT 2	Aargh…
SCOUT 1	My granny missed it. She goes into her cellar when there's going to be a raid.
SCOUT 2	Bet she's kicking herself now. Hey. *(He spots something in the grass)* A button! It's the Bosch commander's button.
SCOUT 1	Huh. Look! *(He holds up a scrap of metal)* Bit of the engine!
SCOUT 2	Swap you.
SCOUT 1	No.
SCOUT 2	What a crowd. Good thing we got here early. Everyone wants some of the Zeppelin.
SCOUT 1	Yeh but it wasn't a real Zeppelin.
SCOUT 2	Was!
SCOUT 1	It was a wooden framed Schutte-Lanz SL11. Any idiot could see that.
SCOUT 2	It was a Zepp! Are you saying we didn't shoot down a Zepp?
SCOUT 1	An SL11 isn't a real Zeppelin. It's just a dirigible gas bag.
SCOUT 2	You're a dirigible gas bag!

They fight, then run off.

MERCURY	The funeral of the German crew of the downed airship was held on Sunday at Potters Bar. Also on Sunday the funerals of Frances Bamford, aged 26, and her sister Eleanor Bamford, aged 12, were held in Essendon. The girls, daughters of Essendon's blacksmith, were killed the same night, 3rd of September, when a second airship jettisoned its

bombs over the village. Frances was killed instantly; Nellie was taken to the County Hospital but could not be saved. Political crisis. Asquith resigns. Lloyd George is PM. Showing now at The Wash Cinema. The Great Battle of the Somme. The greatest drama in which humanity has ever engaged!

CLAUD SWEENEY, in the trenches.

SWEENEY Dear Mum. It's been quite lively here. Ware boys did our bit in the 'Great Push'. I am writing to say I might be getting a medal, but don't worry! I didn't do anything dangerous. We bombed a dugout and, bit of luck, three German officers and 29 men came up from it. Me and my pal disarmed and captured them. We lost our Corporal and so we took command of the bombing post and captured us a bunch of German machine gunners. Oh yeh, remember Albert Hawkes from the Church Lads' Brigade? He's an Acting Company Commander now. It hasn't stopped him singing.

HAWKES sings 'Little Grey Home in the West'.

FREDA, the begonia lady, comes on.

FREDA We're at the third Christmas of the war, but we in the Bengeo Cottage Garden Society are looking ahead to the new season. May I put a request to all of you? In the spring, sow special poppies, which are badly needed for wounded soldiers. Poppies to dull the pain. Remember please – for 1917, grow poppies.

End of ACT 1.

ACT 2

A SAPPER comes on, carrying a spade.

SAPPER   January 1917. Worst blizzards anyone can remember. Telephone lines come down so they've called in the Royal Engineers. We've been out on the Hertford Road waist deep in snow but we kept our spirits up. *(Sings)*

    For one and a penny a day
    Yes one and a penny a day
    We are digging great holes
    And putting up poles
    For one and a penny a day…

(Shivers) This weather. God knows what it's like for the lads at the Front.

ANNIE SWAN, carrying a shopping bag.

ANNIE   There is a word we have all come to loathe this winter. Substitute. We buy substitute butter, eat substitute bread, cook with substitute egg. Soon we will have substitute people. There is a world wheat famine. Our National Food Controller says if we voluntarily limit the amount of bread we eat, the country can avoid compulsory rationing. People aren't going to like it. Bread is the staff of life, and when it is threatened it rouses real indignation – the sort that culminates in revolution. Mind you, what will make people eat less bread is that the new loaves made with substitute flour - barley, oatmeal, heaven knows what - are quite disgusting. However *(she lowers her voice)* for some reason they don't have the same shortages in Scotland. A friend in Dundee sends me a white loaf every week… *(she produces the loaf from her bag and holds it up adoringly)* Made with wheat flour. I don't think I could get through without it.

A friend calls to her from off.

WOMAN   Mrs Burnett Smith! How are you?

ANNIE hastily and guiltily hides the loaf in her bag and greets the friend.

The Tribunal. KINMAN faces a group of tradespeople.

KINMAN Another year, another battle with the butchers of Hertford. I come back from my tour of duty with the 3rd Beds and you're still here. I'd rather face the Germans. Now, between you, you have twelve slaughtermen. The army needs 10 of those men. Two experienced slaughtermen should be quite adequate for a town this size.

BUTCHER You're driving us out of business.

KINMAN If you cannot agree to co-operate you will be forced to do so. You have made four appeals. I do not want to see any more appeals before this tribunal! Now the bakers. Thank God we have no candlestick makers. Gentlemen, the military want eleven of your employees.

BAKER Impossible.

KINMAN Not impossible if you agree to share deliveries. There is no need for a dozen separate delivery boys criss-crossing Hertford and Ware.

BAKER The ladies would complain if they did not have their regular boy.

KINMAN The ladies would understand.

BAKER You're trying to put us out of business!

KINMAN There are many young women keen to do their bit. They could perfectly well make deliveries, or even work in the bakeries.

BAKER Oh no Major! Baking is a skilled trade. It's not the sort of thing a woman could do.

KINMAN No more appeals! When we began I thought the tribunal would only be needed for a few months. How wrong I was. Still, we've sent one thousand, four hundred and seven men to the army. I suppose we've done our job.

ELIZABETH and EMILY are queuing at the grocer's.

ELIZABETH   What you got?

EMILY   Cheese, gone up tuppence since last week. Bacon.

ELIZABETH   Gone up sixpence. Potatoes?

EMILY   Can't find any.

ELIZABETH   Me neither.

EMILY   Not got bread yet because I'm going down the road. He's still selling a loaf for tenpence and the others are tenpence ha'penny.

ELIZABETH   Not any more. He's gone up to tenpence ha'penny too. He's been leaned on, if you know what I mean. Brought into line.

GROCER   Next? Mrs Wilkes, what can I get you?

EMILY   A pound of sugar please and a packet of malted milk biscuits.

GROCER   I'm afraid I can't do that Mrs Wilkes.

EMILY   Rich tea then.

GROCER   No I can't let you have a pound of sugar unless you spend at least seven shillings in this shop.

EMILY   Seven shillings! I only want sugar and biscuits.

GROCER   For my regular customers, such as yourself, I am able to let you have half a pound of sugar if you also buy coffee or tea.

ELIZABETH   What do you mean, 'able'?

GROCER   Sorry ladies, but you know how scarce sugar is.

EMILY   I haven't got enough for tea or coffee. I wasn't going to buy any this week.

ELIZABETH   Look, I want tea. I'll split the sugar with you. Two packets of tea and half a pound of sugar please.

GROCER	You can't do that. It's against the rules.
ELIZABETH	There aren't any rules. You made 'em up.
GROCER	You won't find many shops that'll sell you sugar at all.
ELIZABETH	Do you want my money or don't you?
GROCER	*(With bad grace)* Two packets of tea and half a pound of sugar.
EMILY	And the malted milk.
GROCER	Don't push your luck madam.
MERCURY	Five hundred thousand army substitutes are wanted. A man who will not help his country is helping the enemy. Enrol NOW for National Service. The National Service Scheme headed by Mr Neville Chamberlain has set a minimum wage at 25 shillings a week, so that men should not be asked to work at the low rate prevailing in agricultural areas. Magistrates court report. Mrs Alice Andrews of Stapleford was charged with stealing coal from the new Hertford to Stevenage railway at Bull's Mill. Mrs Andrews stated she had never done anything like that before. Her husband is a ploughman at Waterford Hall Farm, earning eighteen shillings a week. Britain is now spending £5,790,000 a day on the war.

LOUISA PULLER and JENNY MASON have posters, advertising for women land workers.

LOUISA	We should put bills up wherever we can Jenny. The earlier we get our ladies' labour gangs together this year the better. There's more land under the plough now.
JENNY	But not so many women Miss Puller. There's other jobs you can do, better paid.
LOUISA	Not as much fun surely. I hope the women haven't been put off by the attitude of the farmers. Mrs Abel

	Smith has been very annoyed because the girls from her dairy training centre have found it hard to get jobs, even though dairy workers are so scarce. She told the county agricultural committee, 'I realise that it is some sacrifice for farmers to drop their prejudices and employ gels, but what is that inconvenience compared with the great sacrifice that men are making for us on the other side of the water?'

They laugh.

LOUISA	We're being urged to gather herbs again this year. Belladonna and Coltsfoot. We should send the children out for Coltsfoot.
JENNY	What's Coltsfoot for?
LOUISA	Breathing difficulties. For the men who have been gassed. *(Pause)*
JENNY	You must be feeling pleased Miss Puller.
LOUISA	Why?
JENNY	You're going to get the vote.
LOUISA	Oh. That. I'm not counting my chickens. We've had electoral reform proposals before and they haven't come to anything.
JENNY	But this time it's different. For heaven's sake, look what we've been doing in this war. They can't say women ain't fit to vote. You'll get it this time.
LOUISA	You'll get the vote too Jenny.
JENNY	I don't own any property.
LOUISA	You're married and over 30. That seems to be what is required.
JENNY	Don't see why it should make any difference if you're married or not.

LOUISA   So that little feeble female minds will have a man to guide them. Oh I sound bitter. I shouldn't be ungrateful I know. Well, I shouldn't ought to feel grateful or ungrateful! I just can't stand the feeling that we're getting the vote as a reward for good behaviour! *(They both laugh)*

MERCURY   14th of April 1917. So many momentous events have taken place in these weeks that it is hard to take them all in. The Russian revolution, the American intervention in the war, and the new British offensive on the Western Front – all chapters in the greatest drama in human history.

Sound of the Zeppelins going over. Everyone looks up.

PEMBERTON-BILLING calls a meeting at the Corn Exchange, chaired by the Town Clerk, ALFRED BAKER. WILLIAM GRAVESON is there.

P-B   One hundred and fifty people have died in this week's daylight raid on East London. Are we going to sit here and let the Germans kill our children? Mr Chairman, I have already put it to the House of Commons - we need not only a system of air raid warnings but a move to reprisals on Germany!

GRAVESON   Mr Chairman…

ALFRED   No Mr Graveson…

GRAVESON   I wish to speak on these diabolical proposals…

ALFRED   You may not speak Mr Graveson!

GRAVESON   Reprisals – are we to descend to this level and out Kaiser the Kaiser?

ALFRED   Reprisals are recognised in our own code of military law. We must pay back Germany in her own coin, day by day.

P-B   I don't call it reprisals, this is an air offensive. Within a week it would bring the German nation to its knees. The codes of warfare as known in the past are

	of no use when we are fighting for our very national existence.
GRAVESON	Mr Chairman…
ALFRED	Sit down Mr Graveson. We have heard enough from the miserable sentimentalists who are doing their best to lose us the war. This is war, so let it be war to the knife. Would to God Cromwell were here today!
P-B	The only way to protect our women and children at home is by properly organised reprisals. Let us drop six bombs for every one dropped on us!

Mixture of cheers and boos.

GRAVESON	Six British bombs for one German, what does that mean? It means the murder in cold blood of six German babies for one British. We would be killing non combatants – for what? Vengeance? To provoke terror? Mr Chairman, nothing is easier than to appeal to the prejudices and passions of men, nothing is more dastardly… Let those who advocate this brutality do it themselves and take the risks, whether they are Members of Parliament, chairmen who refuse to let opponents speak, or the supporters at the public meeting. To shout and then stop at home, while the youth of the country are compelled to go and do these brutal deeds for them, seems to me the depth of meanness. But then – I am a sentimentalist.

ELIZABETH and EMILY shopping.

ELIZABETH	They say sugar's going to be rationed.
EMILY	I think it will be fairer. At least if we all have a sugar card the shops won't be able to refuse us.
ELIZABETH	They'll find a way. 'I'm sorry madam this sugar card is only valid on the fifth Thursday of the month when the moon is full'. And I've heard you can only get sugar for jam making now if you've got fruit trees.

EMILY	I've got a few raspberry canes out the back. Does that count?
ELIZABETH	I shouldn't think so Emily. Have you got an acre of orchard? Have you got a team of gardeners to tend it? Are you Lady Muck who doesn't need the jam anyway? No sugar for you my girl!
EMILY	I 'spect more stuff will have to be rationed.
ELIZABETH	Have to be. People won't make sacrifices. They're too selfish.
EMILY	We've all got our lives decided for us now. It's fairer, but sometimes I feel we're all in the machine. Still, it's only for the duration I suppose.
ELIZABETH	I suppose.
MERCURY	Have you grown a whopper? The Mercury is launching its Giant Potato competition!

Council meeting, WILLIAM GRAVESON in the chair.

GRAVESON	Welcome to this meeting of the county council committee gentlemen. It is rather hot. Shall we open a window?
CLLR 1	Open a window and maybe we can hear the guns.
CLLR 2	You can't hear the guns in France from here.
CLLR 1	Mr Chairman I wish to raise the matter of our female road sweepers.
CLLR 2	Huh. They are slower than the men, the foreman says.
CLLR 1	They do the work required. From the public's point of view, a road swept by a woman looks exactly the same as a road swept by a man. Yet they are earning substantially less – only fourpence an hour. It is not a living wage.

CLLR 2	It does not need to be. They have husbands.
CLLR 1	They could earn three times as much at the munitions factory.
CLLR 2	That's not our fault – it's the munitions paying ridiculous wages.
GRAVESON	Hm. Report from the licensing committee?
CLLR 1	Er, to be brief the number of pub licences is to be reduced throughout the county. A survey found that in Hertford alone there is one licensed house to every 145 people.
CLLR 2	And you still can't get a decent pint!
CLLR 1	Sadly the committee can do nothing about the fact that the beer is like dishwater.
GRAVESON	Now gentlemen, new legislation being considered will give education authorities like ourselves powers to improve child health.
CLLR 2	What's health got to do with us?
GRAVESON	In my view the path of national safety and prosperity lies along the lines of national health.
CLLR 2	In my view it is not the job of the council to interfere in the home. If children are sickly it's because their parents are not feeding them properly and they're staying up all night to watch for Zeppelins.
CLLR 1	We've been sending the local children to sleep in the Molewood Tunnel if it looks like there might be a raid. I had to convince them the line isn't open yet and they won't be run over by a train.
GRAVESON	It is an education issue. Teachers report that the children aren't concentrating in class because they're hungry.
CLLR 2	The plain truth is that people round here don't know how to manage a household. Do you know only two days ago I saw a girl, one of a family of eight young

	children, taking a large pan of bread crusts to a neighbour's pigs! Those crusts could have made a bread pudding. Our cook does an excellent one.
CLLR 1	Well…
CLLR 2	Income has nothing to do with it. It is the way the money is spent, not the amount which is earned, that matters.
CLLR 1	It's our job to plan for improvement.
CLLR 2	Planning is another word for interfering.
GRAVESON	The country has endured war for three years. Things can no longer be done the way they've always been done.
CLLR 2	People have put up with changes, yes, but only because they know it's just for the duration.
GRAVESON	You're wrong. People think differently now.
CLLR 1	Indeed they do.
MERCURY	In three years we have learned what modern warfare means. Yet, after three years of the most barbarous, bloody and appallingly destructive strife the world has ever witnessed, would any of us wish to retract the vow we made – that rather should England perish than she should prove false to her friends?

Drumming.

MERCURY	Passchendaele. The 31st of July 1917. In the early morning the 1st Hertfordshire regiment under the command of Lieutenant Colonel Frank Page advanced to the attack over the top of the trenches. By 10 o'clock they had captured the village of St Julien and were pushing deep into German territory.

SWEENEY and BILLY, a Drummer, in the trenches. BILLY is playing with his drumsticks. SWEENEY is poised to go over the top.

BILLY	Ready Sweeney?
SWEENEY	Lance Corporal Sweeney to you.
BILLY	Acting lance corporal.

SWEENEY takes a swipe at him. They laugh.

BILLY	Sergeant major says you don't have to go over in the first attack.
SWEENEY	I'm bloody going. Colonel Page goes over the top, me next.

BILLY puts down his drumsticks and picks up his gun.

SWEENEY	What're you doing?
BILLY	I'm going too.
SWEENEY	Drummers are stretcher bearers Billy. You don't have to come.
BILLY	I'm coming with you. Ware boys together eh?

They go over the top. SWEENEY falls.

MERCURY	The Herts Guards. Unflinching unto Death. Frank Page fell early on, hit in the throat – he died instantly. His Adjutant Captain Milne, and then Captain Lowry were killed. The captains, the lieutenants, the second lieutenants, all fell. In the end there was only a sergeant, himself severely wounded, to take charge.
BILLY	It was the severest fighting our regiment has experienced. I was just behind our famous Colonel when he was shot. I am afraid we had a good number taken prisoners, as the Hun counter-attacked and cut some of our men off. I was with Claud Sweeney when he got killed. I expect his mother knows by now. I was hit but managed to crawl back to St Julien village, then got carried to the dressing station by two German prisoners. A few minutes earlier I was shooting at Germans and now I had my arms around two of them as they carried

me down the line. I am shot badly through both thighs, but going on satisfactory.

ELIZABETH reads a letter, news of her son's death.

MERCURY   Casualties on the Home Front. Since the war began, a quarter of a million children have died. Besides this, German bombs on our towns are but a few drops in the bucket. The killed are all under five years of age and they die at the rate of about a thousand a week. The principal causes are slums and overcrowding, dirt, disease; shortage of competent midwifery and nursing; ignorance on the part of young mothers; and last, but by no means least, insufficient nourishment. The public want action to stop these needless deaths. This war has changed attitudes. The corn of things that really matter is being winnowed from the chaff of trivialities.

ANNIE SWAN comes on, followed by people (including children) each carrying a dish of rather grey-looking food.

ANNIE   Welcome to our Food Control Exhibition. Here you will find many ideas for making nourishing food with the means available to us. I am delighted to say we have had many entries for our competition, including some wonderful dishes prepared by children, and the results can be seen here.

MERCURY   Mercury Giant potato competition! We have joint first prize winners. Mr RT Andrews of Castle Street and Mr LG Page of Goffs Oak Hotel, both grew whoppers weighing three pounds one ounce. The potatoes will be donated to the VAD hospital and I'm sure the soldiers will enjoy the mash!

ANNIE   So the winners are: bread made from flour substitute – Mrs Anderson; cake from flour substitute, no egg – Miss Dickins; dishes from meat substitute – we have Miss Martin with nut sausages and Miss Sparks with lentil cutlets; dish prepared from herrings – Miss Burke; dinner for four people to cost not more than one shilling – Ethel Morris. Congratulations everyone! The dishes are for sale and I urge you all to buy one. They will make a delicious tea!

Everyone looks glumly at the food.

Two children come on, TOM and FLO. They have been collecting conkers.

FLO	How many conkers you got?
TOM	Fifty. *(He picks one up triumphantly)* Fifty-one!
FLO	What are they going to do with them?
TOM	They use them in munitions.
FLO	They fire them at the Germans?
TOM	'Spose so.
FLO	Good. I thought they might make us eat them.

Angry FARMER appears.

FARMER	Oi, this is private property. What are you kids up to?
TOM	Nothing.
FARMER	Right. What's in that bag?

The children show him the conkers. He grabs them.

FARMER	And what do you need with so many conkers?
TOM	Council gives you money for them.
FARMER	Does it now? You ain't got any sparrows or rats, have you?
FLO	No sir.
TOM	Why would we want sparrows and rats sir?
FARMER	You know the council pays money for vermin, to protect our food supplies. You'll have to get up earlier in the morning to pull one over me.

TOM	Honest sir, we don't know anything about that.
FARMER	All right then, be off and don't let me catch you on my land again. If the government wants conkers, they're mine to sell, you hear me?
FLO	Yes sir.

The FARMER exits. The kids wait till he's gone, then pick up two bags.

TOM	That was close.
FLO	Never mind, we got lots.
TOM	With a penny per rat's tail and tuppence per sparrow, he can keep his stupid conkers.

They laugh.

A solemn Christmas carol plays.

MERCURY	What would one give to be able, at this season of the year, to offer and receive the old time greeting, 'A merry Christmas and a happy new year'? For we are living in the shadow of a mighty sorrow; the sun has gone down and the night is upon us; we seem to hear the beating of the wings of the Angel of Death; from many of us he has taken those we love best on earth, and we do not know at what moment he may return for others that are near and dear to us. Anniversaries and festivals, which once meant so much to us, are now unreal. They seem to belong to another world and another existence of which we are but dimly conscious and to which we can never return.

WE JOHNS come forward in flying gear.

W E JOHNS	I got my wings and did a stint as a flying instructor. But of course what I really wanted to do was get out to France. By 1918 nothing seemed to be happening. Then I was given a warrant to ferry a De Havilland DH4 to France. This was my chance to get over there. I arrived at the airfield, no DH4. I hung around, crashed a Canadian poker school and two hours later got up from the table completely broke. Luckily I was able to cadge a lift with a chap taking a Handley Page to France and one way and another

I got to 55 Bombing Squadron base. They were crying out for replacement pilots and observers so I was in. The first morning I was there I won nine hundred francs and a revolver from a delivery pilot at two handed pontoon. Things were looking up.

MERCURY   Notices in the newspaper. Second Lieutenant Reg Campkin, only surviving son of Mr and Mrs Campkin of Datchworth, has been killed at Bailleul. Mrs Wilsher of Tewin seeks information concerning her son, Private W Wilsher 18230 2nd Beds regiment. He was reported missing on September 20th last. Any comrade who has seen or heard of him since will earn the mother's gratitude by writing to the above address.

EMILY comes on, weighed down by bags. She queues for the grocers, very fed up.

GROCER   Mrs Wilkes, what can I get you?

EMILY   Ooh, I think I'll have a round of Stilton and a big box of toffees.

GROCER   I'm afraid…

EMILY   I know I know. I'll have my weekly one and a half ounces of tea and four ounces of marg per person as according to the ration card. There's four of us. *(She holds put the cards)* Sugar too.

GROCER   Nothing doing Mrs Wilkes. I have no tea.

EMILY   Coffee then.

GROCER   No coffee, or sugar. And no bacon, before you ask.

EMILY   *(Losing her temper)* What does it say in your window? Get your tea and sugar here. You're a grocers! I'm registered with you – I can't shop anywhere else. I'm registered with you for tea and sugar and YOU HAVEN'T ANY TEA OR SUGAR!

GROCER   It's hardly my fault.

EMILY   What are we going to eat?

GROCER	Don't ask me, ask the Food Control Committee. It looks to me like you've bought something.
EMILY	Only potatoes. We're sick to death of potatoes! I bet the Food Control Committee whoever they are don't live on bread and potatoes.
GROCER	Rationing is much fairer. Everyone gets their fair share of food, including the working people.
EMILY	Except there isn't any food. We're getting our fair share of bugger all!
GROCER	No need for language Mrs Wilkes.
EMILY	The butcher's was closing just as I got there. He had nothing to sell. Well he said he has got meat – he had a delivery of pork and it's hanging in the cold room because he's not allowed to sell it. He has no permission to sell pork this week, only lamb and beef. And he hasn't got any lamb or beef. It's enough to drive you to drink.
GROCER	I wouldn't bother Mrs Wilkes. The pubs have got no beer. How is Mrs Sweeney?
EMILY	She's gone to Ball's Park today. There's a presentation.

ELIZABETH SWEENEY facing KINMAN. He presents her with a medal in a box.

KINMAN	Mrs Sweeney. I have the honour and pleasure of presenting you with the Military Medal won by your son Claud in November 1916 for gallantry at the Battle of Ancre. I sincerely regret that your son lost his life in the defence of his country and that he is not here in person. The NCOs in training here at Balls Park join me in congratulating you on such a brave son.

'Three cheers for Claud – hip hip hoorah' etc.

ELIZABETH	Thank you Major, sir.

KINMAN   I understand you also lost your husband Mrs Sweeney.

ELIZABETH   John, yes. In 1915.

KINMAN   You have certainly done your bit Mrs Sweeney.

ELIZABETH   Me? What have I done?

KINMAN   You have sacrificed those most dear to you.

ELIZABETH   Yes but I didn't want to.

KINMAN   Victory is within our grasp because of men like them.

ELIZABETH   I don't care about victory I want my son back!

MERCURY   The Great German Offensive. Splendid British Resistance. The Britisher by repute is at his best when put on his mettle. Now for the second time in this war our army – and when we say the army we mean the whole nation – is in a tight corner. It is retreating. The enemy says it is beaten. But we shall fight on with our backs to the wall.

ANNIE   The idea came up of communal kitchens. Towns would set up a central kitchen, as a business, not a charity, supplying a large number of meals at smallest cost. As chairman of the Hertford Kitchen Committee, I played my part in getting ours up and running.

MERCURY   A central kitchen will be opened for the public at the Corn Exchange, Hertford, on Wednesday January the 23rd by the Mayor. All who wish to help the authorities solve the food difficulty should buy from this kitchen, which will be open from 11.30 am to 2pm each day (Sunday excepted). The prices will be the lowest possible. Suitable vessels must be brought for the meals, which will not be consumed on the premises.

People gather for the kitchen, bringing bowls and plates.

WOMAN   What have we come to. Queuing for a soup kitchen.

MAN   It's not a soup kitchen Sarah.

WOMAN   *(Pointing to menu)* Soup. Penny ha'penny.

MAN   Yes and roast beef, fourpence. Beef steak pudding, fourpence. Shepherd's pie thruppence. Veg a penny a portion. Rice pudding, penny ha'penny. Guard's pudding, thruppence.

WOMAN   What's Guard's pudding?

MAN   Lovely. It's got raspberry jam in it. Try it.

WOMAN   Alright. I might have the shepherd's pie first.

ANNIE   The idea caught on, there were regular queues outside the door. Roast meat quickly became unobtainable and after the first month it was meat puddings only, but people were better fed because of the kitchens. The children certainly were. As it happens, I was not at the opening of the Hertford kitchen. I had travelled to the United States – on a national mission…

W E JOHNS   We were flying DH4s, nicknamed the flaming coffin because it was so easy to set the petrol tank on fire. On one of my first flights, some silly ass had timed the synchronisation of the gun and the propeller all wrong. So when I fired, I shot my prop into a thousand pieces. Luckily there were plenty of fields handy so there was no difficulty in getting down. Our bombing raids were pretty effective. We were managing to get deep into the Rhineland, did a big daylight raid on Frankfurt. That was a show to be remembered. We also carried incendiary bombs. We didn't like them, but they were good for a little game. We tried to set the German cornfields on fire, but the damn things wouldn't burn. So we tried to set light to a bigger target – the Black Forest. Pretty disappointing results there too.

HAWKES sings in the trenches, to the tune of 'Little Grey Home in the West'.

> In our little wet home in the trench
> That the rain storms continually drench
> There's a dead cow near-by with its hooves in the sky
> And it gives off a terrible stench.
> Beneath us instead of a floor
> Is a layer of cold mud and some straw.
> The Jack Johnsons we dread
> As they speed overhead
> In our little wet home in the trench.

Explosion. HAWKES is knocked down.

WILLIAM GRAVESON and MRS GRAVESON at the breakfast table, reading the paper.

GRAVESON	Pass the toast dear. Poor Albert Hawkes.
MRS G	Not dead?
GRAVESON	No. Severely wounded it says, in hospital.
MRS G	Such a lovely voice. I hope he's alright.
GRAVESON	Oh no… *(He groans and puts the paper down)*
MRS G	Dear! What is it?
GRAVESON	That man!
MRS G	Which ma… oh Pemberton-Billing. Is he dead?
GRAVESON	Unfortunately not. He's in court, dragging the name of Hertford into further disrepute.
MRS G	That business. It's got nothing to do with us.
GRAVESON	No but a good few Hertford people have got themselves embroiled in it. Our fool town clerk Alfred Baker is Treasurer of the ridiculous organisation Billing calls his party – the 'Vigilantes'. I really don't think it's proper for Baker to be involved with that kind of politics. They publish a nasty little magazine, expounding Billing's increasingly demented views and now they have this libel case.

MRS G	I don't understand it at all. He was rude about some actress and she's suing?
GRAVESON	Something like that.
MRS G	What did he say that was so bad?
GRAVESON	Er, he accused her of, of being…. Well I don't like to say, it was highly improper.
MRS G	I thought he accused her of being a lesbian?
GRAVESON	Er, yes, well, and more…
MRS G	Oh if you won't tell me I shall have to ask Cook. She reads the Daily Mail.
GRAVESON	Billing doesn't really care about Maud Allen, he just wants a platform for his theory about the Hidden Hand, some sort of unseen force in the government of this country which is bent on losing us the war.
MRS G	Let me see.
MERCURY	Repeated reference was made to the 'German Black Book' containing forty-seven thousand names of English people and quite a sensation was created when it was stated that the Judge's name was on the list, and also those of Mr and Mrs Asquith, Lord Haldane and other prominent personages.
GRAVESON	Mad.
MRS G	Who are these forty-seven thousand people?
GRAVESON	They're supposed to be people with some sort of guilty secret, who are open to blackmail and therefore in the grip of the Germans.
MRS G	It's an awful lot, forty-seven thousand. The Hand can't be terribly well Hidden. Are you on the list dear?
GRAVESON	I shouldn't be at all surprised. And the editor of the Mercury. Billing has never liked him either.

MRS G   Well it's all very silly. And nothing to do with the
                 war. I'm sure he'll be laughed out of court. Poor
                 Alfred Baker. His son Wilfred is a prisoner of war in
                 Germany you know. And now the other son's been
                 wounded.

ANNIE   I received an invitation from Colonel John Buchan,
                 fellow Scot, fellow writer and now director of the
                 Ministry of Information, to go to America on a
                 mission for food. My job was to tell the American
                 people what we had done in the war and to impress
                 on them how urgently we needed the produce they
                 alone could send. Britain had only six weeks supply
                 of food left. The first meeting I addressed was in
                 New York, in a gorgeous Fifth Avenue mansion.
                 Never shall I forget that audience, their pearls alone
                 would have financed any decent war. After that I
                 went to Washington to consult with the head of food
                 administration, Herbert Hoover. As soon as I got to
                 his office he said: 'I've got 200 food administrators
                 from every state in the union next door. Come in and
                 tell them what you want.' I was terrified but I told
                 them. Within a few minutes I was booked up to visit
                 so many states that I saw myself stranded in
                 America for the duration.

Rally of land workers, flags and 'Song of the Land Army'. LOUISA PULLER in a good mood.

LOUISA   This is our great recruiting rally. Women of Britain –
                 the nation's food supply needs you! Summer is here
                 – get out in those fields. We're pulling out all the
                 stops today. Starting at the Great Eastern station in
                 Hertford, we're going to have a procession headed
                 by the buglers from the Grammar OTC. The Scouts
                 and Girl Guides have turned out to march with us
                 and the land army gangs from all over the district
                 are here in force. We've got Standon over there – my
                 bunch. Sawbridgeworth. Tewin. Watton at Stone.
                 The London contingent have come back for their
                 second year. And when we've done our procession
                 and signed up some new recruits I hope, we're
                 getting back on the train, heading down to
                 Broxbourne and doing it all again, to get that lot
                 down there signed up for healthy outdoor work.
                 Although I think they are rather attached to their

unhealthy but lucrative toil at the munitions in Waltham Cross.

Song of the Land Army (to the tune of The British Grenadiers):

> Our women all are working, in many diverse ways.
> None ever dream of shirking, nor ask for fame and praise.
> There are many women's armies, but none do work so grand,
> As they plough and sow and reap and mow,
> Our women on the land.

ANNIE   It was an adventure, my long and strenuous campaign from the Atlantic to the Pacific coast. State after state mobilised to send food to Europe. Some places were a little more difficult. I arrived one afternoon at a township in Ohio. I knew it would not be easy when I saw that every single name above the shops on main street was German. The mayor reluctantly allowed me to speak at an event. Before me was a serried row of highly upholstered Germanic women. They were the front line. I went for pathos, never mentioning the Kaiser or criticising the 'enemy', but talked of war as a menace to all societies. I vowed to myself I would make these Teutonic matrons shed some tears for the woes of the world or perish in the attempt. Incredibly, I succeeded and sat down to rapturous applause.

MERCURY   Billing acquitted in libel case. Animated scenes in court and outside.

PEMBERTON-BILLING appears, acknowledges applause, surrounded by supporters trying to shake his hand.

P-B   Thank you… thank you… a great day… justice has been done. Ladies and gentlemen – my thanks go to the jury, true Englishmen all – for having the courage to defy the enemy and to recognise where truth lies.

HECKLER   Truth? My arse.

P-B	Do I hear an unbeliever?
HECKLER	Show us this Black Book then, if it really exists.
P-B	It exists and for the security of this nation it must never see the light of day.
HECKLER	Do you really think the government are in the pay of the Germans?
P-B	Why else are we so far from victory despite the valiant efforts of so many brave men? Ladies and gentlemen – the German menace is not on the other side of the Channel. It is here, in our very midst. The enemy is within! They are all in league – the government, the press and above all the Jews! But I will expose their conspiracy. The British people have suffered in silence long enough! I am holding a meeting at the Albert Hall to call for the internment of all aliens *(cheers)* and secure Britain for the British people! *(cheers)*

SCOUT comes on with placard for the WARE AEROPLANE. EMILY stops to look.

EMILY	Has Ware got an aeroplane?
SCOUT	Not yet. We're going to buy one.
EMILY	How much does one cost?
SCOUT	Fifteen thousand pounds missus.
EMILY	You're going to have to collect an awful lot of waste paper for that.
SCOUT	It's not the Scouts, it's national savings week. If people in Ware buy enough war bonds, the air force will name a plane after the town.
EMILY	That's nice.
SCOUT	Yeh, and then it'll be in the paper. Ware defeats the Red Baron! Twenty German planes shot down by Ware. Nyyyoooow takka takka takka .

EMILY	I see.
SCOUT	Better go and buy a war bond missus. Do your duty. Nyyyooow…
W E JOHNS	Back home the politicians were making great speeches about 'our boys', the wonderful spirit of self-sacrifice which must bring us glorious victory. Self-sacrifice my hat. With most of us the war was a personal matter. Another fellow shot at you and you shot back; you shot at another fellow and he shot back and it jolly well served you right. Our target was the railway lines at Mannheim. My petrol tank was hit and there I was, in a petrol-soaked machine, sixty miles from base, my observer killed and my plane being shot to pieces. I crash landed in a field. I have no idea why I didn't burn to death.
MERCURY	The Alien Peril. The government has at last decided to isolate the alien enemy. The temper of the country is becoming ugly. It is considered imperative to maintain order by removing to a safe retreat all Germans domiciled here without distinctions of class. Public opinion wants to see these alien enemies behind barbed wire, not merely the poor waiters and hairdressers, but the people in high social positions who would turn against us at the first opportunity.

ANNIE and LOUISA at a meeting.

ANNIE	Do they mean the royal family?
LOUISA	Oh Annie!
ANNIE	The Saxe-Coburg Gothas?
LOUISA	They're the Windsors now.
ANNIE	What?
LOUISA	While you were in America they changed their name.

ANNIE	Well, this is like old times isn't it? Our suffrage meetings.
LOUISA	I always knew we would get there in the end. But of course, now it doesn't feel like the most important thing in the world any more.
ANNIE	It's not just the vote Louisa, it's everything that goes with it. That's why we're here today.
LOUISA	*(Sighs)* Only if it just comes down to a choice in the election between that Pemberton-Billing and Mr Barnard… I like Mr Barnard. He's always backed the women. But he's just another man in charge, isn't he?
ANNIE	One day women will be MPs too.
LOUISA	You should stand for Parliament Annie.
ANNIE	Och nonsense. *(Addresses the meeting)* Ladies, welcome to the inaugural meeting of the Hertford and Ware Branch of the National Women Citizens' Association. For citizens is what we now are. Full citizens of Britain. A general election is coming and we will be voting for the first time. I believe we can congratulate ourselves on obtaining this tremendous political power. But we should also understand the responsibility. We have this power at the very moment of our nation's greatest need. We must use it to create a new society when the war is over, that is healthier, happier and better in every way.
W E JOHNS	Things didn't go well when I was captured. Some days before, a DH4 had dropped bombs on a village near to where I had landed, killing many children in Sunday school. They blamed 55 Squadron, and me. I was kept that night in a cellar under the schoolhouse, with the body of my dead observer, while the children of the village, whose friends had been killed, gathered outside.

EMILY meets the SCOUT.

EMILY	Did we raise enough money for an aeroplane?

SCOUT	Enough for two aeroplanes!
EMILY	Well, the Terries are winning on the Somme now.
SCOUT	I know. They've broken through the Hindenberg line!
EMILY	We might not need an aeroplane. The war might be over soon.
SCOUT	Oh no missus, I hope not!
MERCURY	The Board of Trade has issued the following notice. The miners have been called up. Our coal reserves have been sacrificed to save the armies and bring the Americans to the front. That decision, grave as it was, has been splendidly justified. The Americans are pouring over. Victory is on its way. The message now to the home front is: use less coal.
W E JOHNS	I was taken to the nearest German army HQ where they tried to pump me for information. They told me I would be shot for bombing undefended towns. The next few days I expected every morning to be taken out for the dawn walk, but it never happened. Instead I was sent to a POW camp near Munich. I managed to escape once. Wandered about for five days, cold and hungry. I think I was glad when a farmer with a shotgun finally caught me in his orchard.

EMILY at the GROCER's.

GROCER	Good news eh Mrs Wilkes?
EMILY	You've got cheese?
GROCER	Belgium liberated. The Huns are in full retreat now. Austria's given in.
EMILY	Oh yes. *(She sneezes)* Excuse me.
GROCER	Are you alright?
EMILY	Just a cold. It's hard to keep warm at home now.

GROCER	You should go to bed Mrs Wilkes. It's probably the influenza.
EMILY	It's just a cold.
GROCER	Go to the chemist and get potassium permanganate. You gargle a weak solution of that with a little salt.
EMILY	Are you turning doctor, now you've no food to sell? I've got a cold, that's all.
GROCER	People are dying from the influenza right, left and centre.
EMILY	Well I know and the schools have been closed for a fortnight to stop it spreading, so I've got the children at home.
GROCER	The daughter of one of my customers came down with it last week. She was a nurse at the VAD hospital. Lovely, strong girl. Dead in three days.
EMILY	Oh. *(Sneezes)* I'm alright.
GROCER	Let's get this war done with and we'll all feel better eh?

Music.

MERCURY	The war is over. So great is our relief, so deep our thankfulness, that it is beyond human expression. Four years ago, Britain set her hand to the plough, and the spirit of the nation has never faltered. All that her sons fought and died for in the world carnage has been achieved; the blood of our heroes, on land and on sea, has not been shed in vain. The nightmare of the past four years will never return. Wrongs will now be righted and militarism will be relegated to the dusty archives of the past. For the sake of the future, Germany must be taught the lesson it deserves. We cannot afford to have the fire, which we have extinguished with the blood of a million of our sons, kindled anew. No, never again!

People come out with flags, somewhat tentatively at first. Whispers of 'is it true?'

WILLIAM GRAVESON steps out, holding a telegram.

GRAVESON   I can announce that at eleven minutes past eleven this morning, the eleventh of November 1918, the armistice was duly signed. The guns have ceased. The war is over.

Celebrations begin. Music, singing, flags, fireworks. People dance and drink. The FARMER greets GRAVESON, a pint in his hand.

FARMER   Here's to peace and ... better beer. Apparently there's a thousand training soldiers heading down into Hertford from Ball's Park.

GRAVESON   I hope it doesn't get too rowdy.

FARMER   Ha, remember the celebrations at the Relief of Mafeking? This is nothing in comparison.

GRAVESON   Eighteen years ago. That seems like another world now. We had everything to celebrate then and no reason to sorrow.

The festivities continue.

The crowd disperses. The music becomes a Christmas carol, 'It Came Upon a Midnight Clear'.

LOUISA PULLER and JENNY MASON meet, both carrying parcels.

LOUISA   Happy Christmas Jenny.

JENNY   Happy Christmas Miss Puller. This year we can really say it like we mean it, can't we.

LOUISA   We can. Did you vote Jenny?

JENNY   I did. Are you disappointed?

LOUISA   Why?

JENNY   You didn't want that Mr Billing to get in again, did you?

LOUISA   Well. In a democratic ballot you have to accept the outcome.

JENNY   I just wonder if voting really matters. It hasn't got us any food or coal has it?

LOUISA   You mustn't think like that Jenny! Having the vote doesn't mean only that you cast a ballot every four years or so. It means that you're a full adult citizen and this country belongs to you as much as it does to the men.

JENNY   Alright and it sounds good when you say it Miss Puller. But who's going to take any notice? It's not just voting, it's everything Miss Puller. What was the point of all that work? Did we ever do any good?

LOUISA   Of course we did. We got people fed. We achieved so much.

JENNY   I know we felt proud of ourselves. But did we do more than take the place of the men so that they could go off and die? If I was one of those men's wives I don't know that I'd thank us. *(Pause)* Happy new year Miss Puller.

LOUISA   Happy new year Jenny.

W E JOHNS come forward, dressed in ragtag bits of uniform.

W E JOHNS   We prisoners were jubilant when we heard of the Armistice. But it wasn't until the thirtieth of November we were loaded into trucks and taken across the lines at Nancy. We had to be debriefed. So I didn't get to Calais until the 23rd of December. I arrived home to my wife and family on Christmas Day. Although I didn't know it, I had been reported 'missing' and given up for dead. When I walked through the back door, the parlourmaid dropped a pan of potatoes and fainted. She thought I was a ghost. Some while later, I went back to Hertford Grammar and saw the Head, Major Kinman. He told me of the names of the Grammar boys who had gone to war and would not be coming back. He had tears in his eyes.

(He reads from a list).

> Huggins, Robinson, Kronenberger, Long, Dellow, Fowler minor, Wells, Phillips (former head boy), Lawrence, Brewster, Ives, Whybrew, Davies, Gray, McClellan, Hammond, Atkins, Fowler major, May, Page DSO, Stearn DSO Croix de Guerre (former head boy), Cooper, Le Blond, Barker, Donovan MC, Campkin, Findlay, Squires, Sharp, Currell MM, Everett (former head boy), Fitch MC, Prior, Duesbury, Harding, Robertson.

Darkness. Light only on ANNIE.

ANNIE   I lost a son. My dear Edward. Not in the conflict but in 1910. It was September, the last day of the summer holidays. He was packing to go back to school. His father had given him a small rifle and as he was putting that in his bag it went off. It was loaded… I rushed in when I heard the shot and found him. He only lived half an hour. It was a senseless accident. There is nothing like the pain of losing a child. It never heals. And when the war came and so many people suffered that loss, I understood how they couldn't face it and sought refuge in meaning. Sacrifice, noble, hero – all the words we use to mask the pain. We all told ourselves it was a sacrifice. We were ennobled by war, war brought out the best in men, in the British people. As if there were no better way of bringing out the best. The soldiers knew it was a lie, but it was a brave man who said so. We began believing our own lies. Anything to stop us looking the war in the face. That gaping, revolting wound which has never healed. Yet somewhere, deep within, there was not a lie. During those four long years, those of us at home – and perhaps the men at the front – were driven by a stern, deep resolve to see the thing through, so that the peace of the world might be secured for all time. That so much self-denying effort should come to naught.

I remember a day in 1916 when my husband, far too old for active service, had nevertheless got himself attached to the Black Watch and was leaving for Gallipoli. Unable to sleep that night, I had a vision of a great Judgment Seat, where kings and emperors, diplomats, politicians, wire-pullers and profiteers will have to answer to the blood-stained hosts they ordered forth to fight and die; a host reinforced by all the women whose hearts had been wrung and broken. It is a vision which some day, somewhere, surely will materialise.

THE END

Some of the historical characters in the play:

Acting Lance Corporal Claud Sweeney
Ware schoolboy and scout. Enlisted with the 1st Herts Territorial Regiment aged 17. Awarded the Military Medal. Died at St Julien, 1917.

Private Percy Huggins
Ware and Hertford Grammar schoolboy; among the first to enlist with the 1st Herts in August 1914. Killed Christmas Day 1914.

W E (Bill) Johns
Born in Hertford; scholar at Hertford Grammar (now Richard Hale School). Pilot in the Royal Flying Corps. Author of the Biggles stories.

Annie Swan CBE
Novelist and journalist, Suffragist. Stood unsuccessfully for Parliament as a Liberal candidate in Glasgow in 1922. Married to Jim Burnett Smith, GP and Hertford town councillor.

Louisa Puller
Cambridge maths graduate; artist; secretary of the Eastern Counties Federation of the National Union of Women's Suffrage Societies.

William Graveson
Magistrate; town and county councillor; Quaker. Co-owner of haberdashery shop which became Graveson's department store in Hertford.

Corporal Alfred Burt
Educated at Cowbridge School, Hertford. Joined the 1st Herts Terriorials in 1911. Awarded the Victoria Cross for conspicuous bravery.

Noel Pemberton-Billing
Independent MP for East Herts 1916-1921. Pilot, inventor and founder of aviation manufacturing company.

Major George Kinman
Headmaster of Ware Grammar and then Hertford Grammar School. Established the school's officer training corps. Chair of Hertford military tribunal.

THE MARCH

Votes *for* Women

By Kate Miller

Two very dynamic women, who appear in *Seeing It Through*, led me to write *The March*.

Annie Swan and Louisa Puller were leading members of the East Herts Women's Suffrage Society. Before researching *Seeing it Through*, I had never heard of suffrage societies, but it was clear that this organisation was the bedrock on which women in East Herts built a programme of highly effective action during the war. These Suffragists were organised and proactive. They were also very civic and community minded, which contrasted with the stock image of the suffragette chaining herself to railings.

Somehow the story that came down over the years is that only 'suffragettes' campaigned for the vote. The militant members of Emmeline Pankhurst's WSPU (Women's Social and Political Union) captured the headlines in the early 1900s and have held attention ever since. That there were many more thousands of women up and down the country lobbying politicians, holding public meetings and trying to persuade their families and communities, slipped out of sight.

The well-known suffragette slogan 'Deeds not Words' was a dig at the non-militant Suffragists, members of the groups which together formed the National Union of Women's Suffrage Societies, headed by Millicent Garrett Fawcett. In the opinion of the WSPU, all the 'words', the lobbying, speaking and letter writing, were ineffective and pointless. But I'm always interested in the people who have been pushed to the side of history. Rather than tell the familiar story of militant martyrdom, I wanted to question it.

Georgina, Cissy, Edith and Jayanti in *The March* are fictional characters, but are based on the activities of real people and their story takes place against a backdrop of actual events in the period 1910-1918. Lady Constance Lytton's courageous story is very much real and her words in the play are largely taken from her own writing.

Early on in my research I came across mention of the women's pilgrimage of July 1913. At first I could find little about it. Apparently this too was an event which had faded from view, until the publication in 2018 of Jane Robinson's excellent book *Hearts and Minds, The untold story of the Great Pilgrimage and how women won the vote*. The fact that this march came though Hertfordshire down two routes became the centre of the play.

Another element was also enabled by new research. Sumita Mukherjee's book *Indian Suffragettes* revealed the extensive links between British suffrage campaigners and Indian women seeking greater social equality.

By organising a national march to present their arguments and demonstrate mass support, the Suffragists created a model of peaceful protest which has reached out round the world. It is fascinating to think how the efforts of ordinary women – efforts derided at the time for being futile – created ripples which changed history.

Kate Miller

The March was first performed at Hertford Theatre on 6 September 2018 with the following cast:

CISSY WALTERS	Catherine Forrester
GEORGINA WALTERS	Lindsay Cooper
EDITH FARMER	Melissa Parker
JAYANTI BANNERJEE	Ninaz Khodaiji
CONSTANCE LYTTON	Paula Tappenden
HARRIET	Paula Tappenden
ALICE	Paula Tappenden

Director	Richard Syms
Musical Director	Christina Raven

ACT 1

SCENE 1

June 1910. Dawn. A golf course in East Hertfordshire. CISSY WALTERS and EDITH FARMER, both aged 15, enter, both carrying a spade and Edith carrying a bundle of poles, with green, violet and white 'Votes for Women' flags on them. CISSY looks around and chooses a spot.

CISSY   Here.

EDITH is looking around nervously and gives a sudden jump and whimper.

CISSY   What?

EDITH   I heard something!

CISSY   There's nobody around Edith. Not even the maddest golfers are out at four in the morning.

EDITH   I did hear something.

CISSY   A pheasant. Look look. This fairway is perfect.

EDITH   Ooh the grass is like velvet.

CISSY   It won't be velvet by the time we've finished. Right!

EDITH gets her spade and is about to start digging.

CISSY   No no!

EDITH   Oh?

CISSY   We can't just dig any old how. I'll mark it out.

She tries to mark big letters on the ground but doesn't get very far. EDITH counts off the letters on her fingers.

EDITH   V – O – T – E – S - F – O – R - W – O – M – E – N. It's going to take ages.

CISSY   Better get a move on then.

EDITH   And it'll be daylight soon.

CISSY   Mm.

EDITH	Suppose we just do V F W.
CISSY	They won't understand.
EDITH	We could make the letters extra big.
CISSY	Golfing men are quite stupid. Papa says.
EDITH	Let's pin a pamphlet to the clubhouse door so they know what VFW stands for.
CISSY	Good idea. Come on – the sun's almost up.

She scrapes out a huge VFW and they start digging. It is harder than they expect. CISSY is determined but EDITH stops.

EDITH	Cissy this is hopeless.
CISSY	Put your back into it!
EDITH	The ground is too hard.
CISSY	You only have to take off the top layer of turf.
EDITH	I can't…
CISSY	Edie! You know how important this is!
EDITH	Yes but…
CISSY	Men have ignored us long enough! They don't care about women but they do care about their precious East Herts golf club and we're going to show them that if they trample on our freedom we can trample on their green!
EDITH	Gosh.

CISSY starts digging with a reckless anger but achieving little.

EDITH	Tell you what Cissy. Let's just do the flags.
CISSY	Alright.
EDITH	They'll be greeted by Votes for Women flying at every hole.

CISSY   We've made a bit of a mess at least.

They kick and scuff the turf a bit more.

EDITH   They won't like it!

CISSY   No! Cry with the wind, for the dawn is breaking!

EDITH   What?

CISSY   March of the Women. The Suffragette song! You know -

She starts singing the first verse of 'March of the Women'. Edith joins in nervously.

CISSY   'Shout, shout, up with your song! Cry with the wind, for the dawn is breaking; March, march, swing you along, Wide blows our banner and hope is waking…'

They run off laughing with flags and spades.

SCENE 2

The Vicarage. CISSY and her mother GEORGINA are in the study. GEORGINA is writing letters and CISSY addressing the envelopes.

GEORGINA   Thirtieth of June 1910. To the Prime Minister… Dear Mr Asquith…

CISSY   Dear Mr Asquith. When are you going to stop being such an ASS and give women the vote? You know you have to…

GEORGINA   Cissy!

CISSY   He does know. Tell it to him straight.

GEORGINA   That's not how things are done.

CISSY   Huh.

GEORGINA   Listen and learn Cissy. Dear Mr Asquith. On behalf of the East Herts Women's Suffrage Society I write to urge your support for the Earl of Lytton's

	Conciliation bill, which seeks to confer the parliamentary franchise on women. On the basis of numerous public meetings held by our society, I can assure you that there is extensive support among both men and women.
CISSY	He doesn't care.
GEORGINA	Politicians like to know what's popular. We shall write to all the Hertfordshire MPs and as many government ministers as possible. We should also write to the Irish Nationalists, since the government's majority depends on them. And these Labour Party MPs representing northern places.
CISSY	They're all for women's suffrage. They say.
GEORGINA	Let's press on. Plenty to be done before this evening's meeting.
CISSY	Not another meeting!
GEORGINA	I'm relying on you Cissy.
CISSY	I was going to play tennis with Edith!
GEORGINA	It's at the Coffee House Tavern in Hoddesdon and there's no-one to put out the chairs.
CISSY	Surely you've got masses of old biddies to help!
GEORGINA	You and Edith will help. It will be an entertaining evening. Annie Swan is speaking.
CISSY	Oh Annie. *(Puts on mock Scottish accent)*. 'Mae husband's the Mayor of Hertford ye ken!'
GEORGINA	*(laughing)* Cissy! That's our chairman you're mocking. She's speaking on 'The vote and married life'.
CISSY	No interest to me then.
GEORGINA	It will be one day.

CISSY	Never. I can't think of anything more boring than married life. Anyway, what's the vote got to do with marriage?
GEORGINA	A lot, unfortunately. Not everyone's husband is as supportive as your father.
CISSY	He's a vicar. Women are his flock.
GEORGINA	The bishop doesn't see it that way. Anyway, some people say married women should not have the franchise, because they are duty bound to vote the same way as their husband, so it's pointless. And some people say *only* married women should have the vote, because they're too ignorant to decide anything without male guidance.
CISSY	Which all proves that some people are complete nincompoops.
GEORGINA	That reminds me. I must tell Cook it will just be Philip and your father for supper tonight.

She leaves the room. CISSY quickly rifles through papers on the desk to find a copy of the newspaper. She scans it hurriedly, peering down the columns. Finds what she is looking for right at the bottom of a page and sighs in disgust. She doesn't notice her mother coming back in and reading over her shoulder.

GEORGINA	'Outrage at East Herts Golf Club?' If it were that outrageous they would have given it more than five lines.
CISSY	Huh.
GEORGINA	'Minor damage to the green was first blamed on badgers, but a pamphlet pinned to the club house door suggests it was the work of militant suffragettes.'
CISSY	What about the flags?
GEORGINA	What?
CISSY	I heard the suffragettes had put flags. In the holes. That's what I heard.

GEORGINA   We don't want militant suffragettes round here.

CISSY   I expect they came up from London.

GEORGINA   No! Mrs Pankhurst has announced a truce while this Bill goes through Parliament. I hope she has finally seen the foolishness of militancy and accepted that constitutional methods are the order of the day.

CISSY   If it gets us anywhere.

GEORGINA   It will Cissy. The Conciliation Bill is real. Earl Lytton has done the right thing in bringing the suffrage supporters from all parties together on this. It will get passed and there won't be any more need for protests and imprisonment. That's all over.

CISSY   Huh. Badgers.

GEORGINA   It's not the Christian way darling, destruction of property.

CISSY   Property? A bit of grass.

GEORGINA   The hallowed turf of a golf course! You know round here that's sacred ground!

They both laugh. GEORGINA spots another announcement in the paper.

GEORGINA   Oh.

CISSY   What?

GEORGINA   Lady Constance Lytton is coming to give a talk at the Temperance Hall.

CISSY   That's wonderful! When?

GEORGINA   I don't think we should go...

CISSY   Ma, we must! Lady Constance Lytton herself...!

GEORGINA   She's speaking about her experiences in prison...

CISSY   She was force fed!

GEORGINA   You're only 15. I don't want your head filled with these degrading things.

CISSY   Papa says we shouldn't close our eyes to human suffering.

GEORGINA   Don't quote your father's sermons at me, my girl.

CISSY   But – Lady Constance!

GEORGINA   I'm not in favour.

CISSY   She's a saint.

GEORGINA   Hm. Saints.

CISSY   I must tell Edith.

GEORGINA   We're not going I said.

CISSY dashes out the door. GEORGINA calls after her.

GEORGINA   Tell Edith we need her on duty tonight. And Cissy, take some of these letters to the post office!

She picks up some of the envelopes and for the first time sees the addresses.

GEORGINA   Mr Herbert 'Enemy of Women' Asquith…
Mr Winston 'Oppressor of the Weak' Churchill…
Mr David 'Ignorant' Lloyd George…!

She goes to the door.

GEORGINA   Cissy! This is not good enough! Come back! CECILIA…!

SCENE 3

July 1910. CISSY, EDITH and GEORGINA are at the meeting at the Temperance Hall.
LADY CONSTANCE LYTTON is speaking. She is nervous but determined and is fighting a cough.

CONSTANCE My first spell in prison, ladies and gentlemen, was a grave disappointment to me. When the medical examination revealed my weak heart, I was whisked off to the hospital wing and looked after much too well, the wardresses addressing me as 'my lady'. This was not the treatment meted out to my sister suffragettes who were put alongside the thieves and pickpockets, despite the fact that our so-called crimes were a political protest. I resolved, not only to share in the sacrifice, but to expose the double standards of the authorities. *(Applause)* I went to Liverpool, a city where I was completely unknown. There I was determined to put ugliness to the test. I cut my hair, bought a long green coat, and a tweed hat - which I jumped up and down on a little - a pair of spectacles and transformed myself from Lady Constance Lytton of Knebworth, sister of the Earl, into plain Jane Warton, seamstress and suffragette. Jane, after Jeanne d'Arc, Joan of Arc. *(Coughs)* Excuse me. On the 14th of January I took part in a demonstration outside Liverpool gaol. I was arrested and charged with obstruction and insulting behaviour. When I was brought before the magistrates I gave my name as Jane Warton and no-one suspected my identity. The magistrates read me a very long and tedious lecture upon the enormity of my offence, an offence which essentially boiled down to – shouting. Following the process with which we are all familiar now, I was fined ten shillings and costs. I refused to pay and was sent to prison for 14 days, third division. Jane Warton received no medical examination. No medical examination! *(Coughs)* I immediately started my hunger strike in protest at being classed as a common criminal. I was put in the punishment cell and after four days without food, on the 18th of January I was subjected to forced feeding. The horror of it was more than I can describe. Afterwards, even worse was the terror with which I anticipated their next attempt. One of the wardresses said – it gets better. She was trying to be kind. They made eight attempts to forcibly feed me, before it became clear my health was suffering. I was released into the care of my dear sister Emily.

Applause.

GEORGINA   Lady Constance. Did your faith give you the strength to undergo such an ordeal?

CONSTANCE It did. I wrote a text from the Bible on the wall of my cell. 'Only be ye strong, very courageous'. I was severely reprimanded for that. And a line from the American Mr Thoreau. 'Under a government that imprisons any unjustly, the true place for a just man or woman is also in prison.'

CISSY   *(to EDITH)* That is so inspiring!

EDITH   Ask her a question.

CISSY   I can't!

EDITH   Go on.

CISSY   Lady Constance.. er.. my lady.. er is there going to be a proper inquiry into your treatment?

CONSTANCE I think not. It has been six months and despite the best efforts of Earl Lytton, the confusion and weakness in our government means any action is unlikely. First of all they declared I was a liar and nothing of this had actually happened. Then they said I was a wealthy attention seeker, who deliberately caused herself to be ill-treated in order to bring the prison service into disrepute. Well, I say I have exposed their lies. The home secretary claimed no distinction was made among suffrage prisoners based on class. Yet Jane Warton, who was guilty of no violence, was placed in the third division in prison. That means hard labour. In Newcastle jail, where I was recognised as Lady Constance Lytton, I had been given a thorough medical examination. Three months later, the prison officers ignored the same heart beating in the same body.

CISSY	But, Lady Constance. Was it exciting being Jane Warton?
GEORGINA	Cissy! Sit down!
CONSTANCE	Jane was a nobody, and she was everybody. After the first feeding, I had the strange sensation of being outside myself, and seeing Jane Warton lying before me. When she had served her time and was out of the prison, no one would believe anything she said. The doctor - when he had fed her by force and tortured her body - struck her on the cheek to show how he despised her. That was Jane Warton, and I had come to help her. *(Coughs and holds on to a chair but gathers herself)* Ladies! Dare to be free! The road ahead demands courage but women have shown that we have that, and more. We have determination. And we have right on our side.
CISSY	Hear hear!
GEORGINA	Ssh!
CONSTANCE	The hunger strikers in Holloway, Strangeways, Winson Green, will not back down. Men have refused to give up power without a fight, but we can fight. We have our weapons. Men have recourse to violence. But women have chosen the weapon of self-hurt to make their protest. It puts great pressure upon the government and we shall prevail!

Applause. CONSTANCE steps down, coughing. The others get ready to go.

CISSY	Isn't she wonderful!
EDITH	She's so brave!
GEORGINA	Brave but misguided. 'Self hurt'. How can ever be a good thing?
CISSY	It's the key Ma. The men in charge cannot stand by when they see women suffering like this.
GEORGINA	I'm not convinced. It's all unnecessary anyway. I'm afraid Lady Constance is out of touch. There's no need to talk of weapons and daring and all those

	Suffragette histrionics when there's a Bill in Parliament which is going to give us what we want. We're not at war with the men.
CISSY	We can't trust politics Ma.
GEORGINA	Politics is how things are done, otherwise why do we want the vote? The National Union of Women's Suffrage Societies has always campaigned through democratic channels, and that has to be the right way.

But CISSY and EDITH are mocking her.

EDITH	Lady Constance had a terrible cough didn't she? They say she's quite ill.
CISSY	It's from the forced feeding. Do you know what they do? They have three people to hold you down and one of them pulls your head back and opens your mouth. Then the doctor pushes a thick tube into your nose and keeps pushing…
GEORGINA	Cissy!
CISSY	There's yards of tube and when it's gone down far enough they put a gag between your teeth and start pouring the liquid food into a funnel and down into your stomach.
EDITH	Euurgh!
GEORGINA	That's enough!
CISSY	It's true! And when they pull the tube out you feel quite stunned and you cough a lot and have an ache in your chest and feel very sick.
GEORGINA	*(Furious)* Be quiet Cissy!
CISSY	Then you sick up all the food so they do it again…
GEORGINA	Just stop it, stop it, both of you! Let's go.

Music.

SCENE 4

November 1910. The Vicarage. GEORGINA at the desk, trying to write. She puts her head in her hands in despair for a while. CISSY enters.

CISSY Not more letters Ma.

GEORGINA Your father's sermon for this week. I'll do the letters this afternoon.

CISSY What's the point?

GEORGINA Maybe I won't write any letters just yet. We're going to hold a branch committee meeting tomorrow to discuss our next steps. Parliament's still in recess. I don't know who to write to.

CISSY They don't take any notice anyway.

GEORGINA But we're so close! Back in the summer I thought we were there. The conciliation bill is ready to be passed, if only the politicians could stop arguing over this budget. Our vote is there – on printed paper – ready to fly.

CISSY If they agree.

GEORGINA I'm certain there will be a majority. Certain.

CISSY It's hopeless.

GEORGINA Nothing is hopeless. Here's Papa's fifteen minutes for Sunday on hope!

She is almost in tears.

GEORGINA Why can't they see how easy it would be to grant us our rights! Forty three years ago John Stuart Mill moved that the voting law be changed so that instead of 'man' it said 'person'. If that had succeeded, women would have the vote on the same terms as men. But, forty three years of arguing…

CISSY I bet they would have found a way to say that a woman is not a person.

GEORGINA   That's all we want to be. A full person.

Pause.

CISSY   There's a march...

GEORGINA   I don't want to hear about it.

CISSY   No but an important one.

GEORGINA   How do you know?

CISSY   Edith's cousin Caroline who's in the WSPU in Kensington.

GEORGINA   We're not taking part in any Suffragette protests.

CISSY   Not a protest. It's the day that parliament goes back. Mrs Pankhurst is having a meeting in Westminster, then they're going to walk to the House of Commons and... I don't know. Make their presence felt.

GEORGINA   With shrieking and shouting and their usual antics.

CISSY   No, it's just women assembling at Westminster, so Mr Asquith can feel us all breathing down his neck. We ought to go.

GEORGINA   Of course not Cissy. It's merely for the Pankhursts' crew.

CISSY   We could go and watch. See what happens.

GEORGINA   We wouldn't be allowed.

CISSY   There's no law against standing in the street. Ma, it will be a historic moment. Just think – if word comes out that Mr Asquith announces there'll be a vote on the bill. Imagine the cheering! It would be wonderful to be there.

GEORGINA   Yes.

CISSY   No more writing letters from Hertfordshire, we'd be on the spot. In London, where it's all happening.

GEORGINA	I suppose we would simply be there to witness.
CISSY	Yes. We must go! Ma? We must.

SCENE 5

Afternoon, Friday 18th November 1910. Near Westminster Abbey. GEORGINA, CISSY and EDITH, warmly and smartly dressed, are standing around, a little unsure, trying to see what is going on.

EDITH	Is anything happening?
GEORGINA	I can't see dear. I'm sure we'll hear when it does.
CISSY	We've been waiting ages! Mr Asquith must have made his speech by now.
GEORGINA	We don't know how things are done in the House of Commons.
CISSY	Huh. We will when women have the vote and there are female MPs and we don't have to just stay here on the sidelines.
GEORGINA	Yes alright Cissy.
EDITH	I'm so cold I can't feel my toes.
GEORGINA	We could go inside Westminster Abbey girls. It might be warmer.
CISSY	Churches are never warm.
EDITH	We could light a candle and huddle round it. *(They laugh)*
GEORGINA	Let's go inside.
CISSY	Not now Mother. We'll miss everything.
GEORGINA	Perhaps afterwards. We can say a prayer of thanksgiving.
CISSY	*(Looking around)* Can you see your cousin, Edie?

EDITH	No. They're meeting at Caxton Hall, she said. I don't know where that is.
CISSY	There's Lady Constance!
GEORGINA	Surely not. She's not well enough to be out on a march.
CISSY	It is her - over there! *(Shouts and waves)* Lady Constance!
GEORGINA	Cissy!

CONSTANCE LYTTON comes over to them. She is frail and has a walking stick.

CISSY	Lady Constance! We saw you speak. You were wonderful.
CONSTANCE	That's so kind.
GEORGINA	We heard you'd been unwell my Lady.
CONSTANCE	Yes. My silly heart you know.
GEORGINA	Should your ladyship be out here in the cold?
CONSTANCE	My health is of no importance compared with what is at stake today.
CISSY	Do you know what is happening? Your ladyship, um…
CONSTANCE	My brother promised to send word out here. I thought we would have heard by now.
EDITH	And they're going to pass the bill?
CONSTANCE	Not today. Today's just the palaver of parliament being recalled. But they'll announce forthcoming legislation and one of those will be my brother's conciliation bill.
GEORGINA	Earl Lytton has done marvellous work…

A noise goes up, a wave of booing and calling.

CONSTANCE   Oh dear.

CISSY   What are they saying?

GEORGINA   I can't hear.

CONSTANCE goes forward to catch what people are saying.

CONSTANCE   Oh no. He's ruined everything…

GEORGINA   No bill?
CONSTANCE   No bill. No parliament.

EDITH   Who?

CISSY   Mr Asquith.

CONSTANCE   The prime minister has just dissolved parliament and the conciliation bill is in the dustbin.

CONSTANCE sags. GEORGINA goes to support her.

CONSTANCE   I must find Emmeline. They're marching here now from Caxton Hall.

EDITH   I'll go with you. My cousin Caroline is there.

CONSTANCE   The word is that Mr Churchill has told the police to stop any women reaching the House.

GEORGINA   Edith I don't think you should…

CONSTANCE coughs and leans on EDITH.

EDITH   I'll be alright.

GEORGINA   Come back here as soon as you see that Lady Constance is safe.

CISSY   I'll go…

GEORGINA   No!

CONSTANCE and EDITH exit.

Another roar from the crowd. CISSY climbs up on a wall to see better.

CISSY   It's the marchers! They're coming down the street, they've got Votes for Women banners. There's millions of policemen.

GEORGINA   I shouldn't have let Edith go.

CISSY   Why are there so many police? Oh it's a wall of black now, I can't see the marchers.

GEORGINA   Can you see Edith?

CISSY   I can't see anything except police helmets. There's horses! The ladies are not giving up! They're trying to push down to the House of Commons but they're getting thrown back. Oh! Oh no…

GEORGINA   What?

CISSY   The police have got truncheons. People are running.

GEORGINA   Where?

CISSY   All over the place.

GEORGINA   We must leave...

CISSY   Not without Edith!

GEORGINA   No. No of course. We'll stay here so she knows where to find us.

The noise of the crowd has grown into screaming and crying.

CISSY   Keep back Ma, the police are lashing out at everyone. There! There's Edith! I think I can see her! Hey Edie!

Before GEORGINA can stop her, she has raced into the crowd.

GEORGINA   No Cissy! Come back!

She rushes after her. The noise of the crowd becomes a cacophony of shouting and shrieking.

Then silence. The light is dim.

GEORGINA staggers back on. Hatless. Her coat and blouse have been ripped open and she struggles to do them up. She sobs.

CISSY and EDITH rush on. They too have lost their hats and look dishevelled but otherwise unharmed. They are laughing and excited.

EDITH	That policeman when Caroline hit him with her brolly!
GEORGINA	Oh thank God! Girls!
CISSY	Ma!

She rushes to her and they hug, GEORGINA wincing in pain but trying not to show it.

CISSY	Are you alright Ma?
GEORGINA	I fell over.
EDITH	We lost our hats. I'm sorry.
GEORGINA	Me too dear.
CISSY	Can you believe it, we got as far as the steps of the House of Commons! You should have been there Ma! There were so many women I thought we were bound to get in, but there were even more police and they stopped us.
EDITH	The policemen were brought in from all over London, someone said. There were hundreds of them.
CISSY	And they used very bad language.
EDITH	In front of ladies!
CISSY	And we found Caroline and she said a group of them were planning to get into the Commons by an underground passage.
EDITH	Like the gunpowder plot.
CISSY	To blow up the Houses of Parliament!
GEORGINA	What a wicked idea.

EDITH	No they weren't going to do any harm. They just wanted to confront the MPs.
CISSY	And tell them they can't drop the bill. It's not fair!
EDITH	But Caroline got arrested.
CISSY	She was dragged off and we tried to grab her.
EDITH	And we couldn't so we…
GEORGINA	What?
CISSY	Nothing.

Pause.

GEORGINA	It's quiet now.
EDITH	Everyone's gone back to Caxton Hall.
CISSY	Or been arrested.
GEORGINA	We must go home.
CISSY	Can't we go to a tearoom?
GEORGINA	For heaven's sake Cissy, how can you think of food? And we'll hardly get served in a tearoom looking like this.
CISSY	I'm starving.
GEORGINA	We'll have something at Liverpool Street station.

She collects herself, struggling not to show pain. Checks she has train tickets etc.

CISSY	*(To EDITH)* Don't let her know we biffed that copper with a placard.
EDITH	Ooh, no…
CISSY	I wish we'd hit him harder!
GEORGINA	Let's go girls.

CISSY   Oh Edie! Best day of my life!

They hug and follow GEORGINA off.

SCENE 6

The Vicarage. July 1911. GEORGINA with her accounts book, CISSY with a pile of receipts. CISSY is singing to herself – 'Little Grey Home in the West'.

CISSY   'When the golden sun sinks in the hills, And the toil of a long day is o'er Though the road may be long, in the lilt of a song I forget I was *weary* before…'

GEORGINA   I know it's popular but must you keep singing that sentimental song?

CISSY   I love it. I need to forget I'm weary…

GEORGINA   Nonsense.

CISSY   Weary of accounts.

GEORGINA   Let's get on please.

CISSY   Third of June 1911 milk deliveries three shillings and ninepence.

GEORGINA   Paid.

CISSY   Seventh of June in the year of Our Lord nineteen hundred and eleven…

GEORGINA   Cissy!

CISSY   Repair of front gate half a crown.

GEORGINA   Yes. Next – two pounds, five shillings and fourpence… Cissy?

CISSY   Eighth of June butcher's delivery two pounds, five shillings and fourpence.

GEORGINA   More expensive than usual… oh yes, the archdeacon came to lunch…

CISSY	Ninth of June delivery of one ton of South African diamonds, three thousand pounds, six shillings and tuppence.
GEORGINA	Cissy!
CISSY	It's so boring!
GEORGINA	The household accounts must be done.
CISSY	Why?
GEORGINA	So that we can live within our means. Which is not always easy.
CISSY	Let me leave school and get a job then.
GEORGINA	You will finish school and attempt to get a place at Girton. I say attempt, since you can't even concentrate on the monthly accounts.
CISSY	What is the point? Either we've got money or we haven't.
GEORGINA	It's not as simple as that. You have to keep control of things. Starting with the household bills. Or else…
CISSY	I don't see why I need to help.
GEORGINA	Because you've got to learn. One day you will have to do this in earnest.
CISSY	Never.
GEORGINA	You will Cissy, when you have a household of your own.
CISSY	I'd rather die.
GEORGINA	Don't be melodramatic.
CISSY	I don't care. You think I dream of having a life as small as yours but I don't!
GEORGINA	You'll feel differently when you're married.

CISSY	I'm never getting married!
GEORGINA	That's childish talk.
CISSY	Because you treat me like a child.
GEORGINA	On the contrary, I'm trying to make you see what it means to be an adult. But you won't help me with the house. You won't take the minutes at the meetings…
CISSY	I'm not going any more. Meetings are no use.
GEORGINA	That is not true.
CISSY	It's either people who already agree with us, or the anti-Suffragists with always the same ridiculous objections. Mocking us. I don't know how you can stand in front of them time after time.
GEORGINA	I can see you've lost interest. Now that there's no progress with the Cause and it's all very dull. Well you have to learn, it's at the dull times that we keep pushing.
CISSY	But all you're doing is talking! And writing more letters to stupid men who ignore us. That's not pushing. It's all utter rubbish!
GEORGINA	Cissy!
CISSY	There's much more we could do but you're the one who's lost interest. You won't let us go to any meetings in London.
GEORGINA	Absolutely not!
CISSY	I'm not allowed to do anything! It's not…

There is a knock at the door.

GEORGINA	Oh. Could that be our speaker?
CISSY	Mary is letting somebody in.

GEORGINA goes out of the room. She comes back in with JAYANTI, who looks resplendent in a colourful sari. CISSY stares.

GEORGINA Mrs Banner…

JAYANTI Bannerjee.

GEORGINA I'm so sorry. Mrs Bannerjee, this is my daughter Miss Walters. Cecilia this is Mrs Bannerjee who will be our guest for the next few days.

JAYANTI shakes CISSY's hand confidently. CISSY is entranced.

JAYANTI It is so kind of you to be my hostess.

GEORGINA We're delighted. I hope you've had a pleasant journey from London.

JAYANTI Yes indeed. And the driver was waiting for me at Ware station. Fortunately he knew exactly where your vicarage is. It is quite… rural round here.

GEORGINA We are a little off the beaten track. Well, you've arrived in time for morning coffee. Oh, perhaps you don't drink coffee Mrs Bannerjee. Would you prefer tea?

JAYANTI Coffee would be lovely.

GEORGINA I thought you might be more accustomed to tea, since… I mean where you come from… you grow it. I mean not you personally…

Pause.

GEORGINA I'm sorry Mrs Bannerjee. I have to confess you've taken us by surprise.

JAYANTI Weren't you expecting me today?

GEORGINA Yes, but they said, 'a lady from India'…

CISSY Not an Indian lady.

JAYANTI I don't understand.

CISSY	We thought you'd be a lady from India, one of these wives of officers retired from the Raj and come back to England. The ones who are always complaining about how cold it is in England and how insolent the servants are.
JAYANTI	Oh.

She bursts out laughing and GEORGINA and CISSY laugh.

JAYANTI	Are there many women like that around here?
GEORGINA	Too many.
CISSY	One wants to say, if you don't like it in England, go back to India.
JAYANTI	No no. We don't want them!
CISSY	I'm not surprised.
GEORGINA	Excuse me.

She goes out of the room.

CISSY	Your sari is beautiful Mrs Bannerjee.
JAYANTI	This is my travelling one.
CISSY	Saris must be wonderful to wear.
JAYANTI	They take practice…

GEORGINA returns with a tray of coffee.

GEORGINA	I've brought this while Mary takes your bag up to the bedroom.
JAYANTI	It's very kind of you to offer me hospitality Mrs Walters.
GEORGINA	Not at all! There's always room in the Vicarage. It was built for a rather larger family than the four of us. We enjoy accommodating our visiting speakers.
CISSY	It relieves the boredom of the village.

GEORGINA   Take no notice of my daughter.

JAYANTI   No no, I have two daughters.

GEORGINA   Have you any sons?

JAYANTI   Three.

GEORGINA   How wonderful! My son Philip goes up to Cambridge in the autumn.

JAYANTI   He must be very intelligent.

CISSY   Pip? Not really. He's a good shot though.

GEORGINA   He's in the officer training corps. They do spend a lot of time on the shooting range. Well Mrs Bannerjee, we're very much looking forward to your address to us tomorrow night. We'll learn all about the Indian Women's Association for…

JAYANTI   The Indian Women's Education Association.

GEORGINA   Mrs Fawcett is a strong supporter of it. She says the best way we can do our duty for the women of India is by helping them to gain an education.

CISSY   Are you a teacher Mrs Bannerjee?

JAYANTI   No but while my husband and I are in London – he is attached to the Indian Office – I wanted to make myself useful. The association suggested I might do a series of lectures to help with fundraising. The money goes towards scholarships for the women who come over from India for their teacher training here. Your network of women's suffrage societies is the ideal means to spread the word.

GEORGINA   Exactly. Women must support each other, and that means across the empire.

JAYANTI   And I wish to learn from you about the suffrage cause too. I am a great admirer of the campaign Mrs Walters.

GEORGINA   I only wish we could show more success.

CISSY	Do Indian women want the vote?
JAYANTI	We have no parliament.
CISSY	Oh.
GEORGINA	You see that is another reason why we must have the vote, so that there can be a female voice in affairs of the empire. Men simply do not think about the tribulations of Indian women, isn't that right Mrs Bannerjee?
JAYANTI	Indeed. Have you been to India Mrs Walters?
GEORGINA	No but I read a lot about it in our suffrage magazine.
JAYANTI	Of course, India was the first civilisation to have true equality between the sexes.
GEORGINA	Oh?
JAYANTI	Indeed, four thousand years ago. Your fight is for the vote but ours is to reclaim the equality that is our natural right.
CISSY	Good for you.

Pause.

GEORGINA	We are expecting a large turnout tomorrow for your talk. Then Cecilia is going to write a report of it for the parish news.
JAYANTI	How wonderful to see mother and daughter working together.
GEORGINA	My husband and son give their wholesale support to women's suffrage too.
CISSY	Not that they actually do anything.
JAYANTI	It can be enough that they don't place obstacles in your way.

GEORGINA   And the following day you're speaking in Letchworth I believe. They're very keen in Letchworth.

CISSY   They wear sandals and eat lentils.

JAYANTI   It sounds like India! Is Letchworth far?

GEORGINA   Not too far. Our branch secretary Miss Puller has arranged for a car to take you there and bring you back. Then the next day the car will take you to Hitchin station.

CISSY   Where are you going next Mrs Bannerjee?

JAYANTI   Manchester! I'm very excited.

CISSY   About going to Manchester?

JAYANTI   The heartland of the women's suffrage campaign! Where Emmeline Pankhurst began.

GEORGINA   Hm. You'll find the Pankhursts aren't in Manchester much these days. They're mostly in London.

JAYANTI   Of course of course. But my belief is the true power of the suffrage campaign comes from the mill workers and shop girls who are the authentic voice of suffering womanhood.

GEORGINA   Oh. I suppose…

JAYANTI   I know this because in India, our fight for equality is in the name of the peasants. What would be the point of educated women bettering their lot if they cannot help their sisters, toiling in the fields. We will be judged on how much we can improve their lives. It is the same here in England.

GEORGINA   Is it?

JAYANTI   Naturally you want the vote but would it change your lives? Your lives are already pleasant. But when the mill girl in Manchester has the vote she can transform her life of drudgery into one of fulfilment!

Pause.

CISSY — Well, lots of women would like fulfilment.

JAYANTI — But wealthy ladies like you already have all you need.

GEORGINA — We're hardly wealthy!

JAYANTI — Compared to a peasant in Bengal you live like queens.

CISSY — I suppose but…

GEORGINA — The purpose of getting the vote is to improve all women's lives, Mrs Bannerjee. We're not blind to the problems. You should see some of the cottages in this very village – earth floors, no running water, children sickly. Men seem happy to ignore such things but women are not. When we all have the vote, vicar's wives and mill girls, the politicians will have to listen to us and do something.

Awkward pause.

GEORGINA — Coffee?

JAYANTI — Thank you.

GEORGINA — How did you get involved with the women's education association Mrs Bannerjee?

JAYANTI — Well I am privileged to know Mrs Naidu. Her sister received one of the first scholarships to come to England.

CISSY — Who's Mrs Naidu?

GEORGINA — Cissy!

JAYANTI — Mrs Sarojini Naidu – the famous poet. She is an inspiration to us all.

CISSY — Ah.

JAYANTI I'm sure you've heard of her. She is very well known in English literary circles. Mr W B Yeats praises her poetry.

CISSY We don't really move in literary circles.

GEORGINA That's not true at all! I can tell you Mrs Bannerjee, the chairman of our own suffrage society is a well-known novelist, Annie Swan.

JAYANTI How marvellous. What does she write?

CISSY Improving novels for ladies.

GEORGINA They're very well written and uplifting.

CISSY And long.

GEORGINA And Mrs Overton, our deputy secretary, is a literary critic who has had two novels published.

JAYANTI Oh you are so cultured!

CISSY In a worthy sort of way.

JAYANTI What do you like to read Miss Walters?

CISSY Rider Haggard. King Solomon's Mines, that's a good one.

GEORGINA And Mrs Naidu is interested in the British suffrage movement?

JAYANTI Of course! She says whether you are demanding the vote, as here in Britain, or education, as in India, the principle is the same – 'the demand of woman to fulfil her destiny!' So when we came to London she gave me a letter of introduction to Mrs Fawcett.

GEORGINA Oh. You have met Mrs Fawcett.

JAYANTI I have been so impressed by the boundless energy of the campaigners. So many marches and speeches. Were you at the great procession of Suffragists for King George's coronation last month?

GEORGINA   No we, er…

JAYANTI   It was a truly international occasion! And all these imaginative campaigns! What did you do to evade the census?

GEORGINA   We didn't actually…

JAYANTI   My friends in London had a midnight supper party on Wimbledon Common! Just so that they could say they were not at home on the night of the third April and cheat the census. No vote no census!

CISSY   And, and I heard Miss Wilding Davison hid in a cupboard in the House of Commons all that night.

JAYANTI   It's true! Until a cleaner found her in the morning! The woman has such daring.

GEORGINA   Dodging the census was a Suffragette idea and nothing more than a prank really.

JAYANTI   But the Suffragettes are in the newspaper every day.

GEORGINA   Maybe. But my belief is, you do not achieve your full rights as a citizen by evading your civic duties. I feel the same about breaking the law and destroying property. How will that demonstrate that women can be trusted with responsibility?

Pause.

JAYANTI   I understand that argument. I would never condone law breaking myself Mrs Walters.

Pause.

JAYANTI   And how old are you Miss Walters?

CISSY   Please call me Cissy. I'm sixteen.

JAYANTI   It's good to see a girl so dedicated to a cause.

CISSY   I'm determined that when I'm 21 I shall have the vote. Or even if it takes till I'm old. Till I'm 50!

JAYANTI	Goodness, let's hope not! I'm thinking Mrs Walters, perhaps Cissy could come with me to Manchester.
GEORGINA	What?
CISSY	Ooh…
JAYANTI	It would be an excellent experience for you to see the true breadth of the campaign.
GEORGINA	I don't want Cecilia attending any Suffragette meetings.
JAYANTI	It will be perfectly respectable Mrs Walters.
GEORGINA	Manchester is a big city. She's not ready for that.
CISSY	We went to Lon…
GEORGINA	NO.
JAYANTI	She could attend the meeting at Letchworth.
GEORGINA	Letchworth. I'm afraid not.
CISSY	It would be educational.
GEORGINA	Your father doesn't want you gallivanting around.
CISSY	I'll ask him…
GEORGINA	It's his responsibility to see you don't come to any harm.
CISSY	But what harm…?
GEORGINA	Your father says no Cissy. That means no.

Pause.

GEORGINA	Shall I ring for more coffee?

SCENE 7

CISSY and EDITH conspiring together.

CISSY … And Mrs Bannerjee knows the Pankhursts and she's met Miss Wilding Davison.

EDITH Gosh.

CISSY And her husband's something at the Indian Office, he's probably terribly important, and she showed me her best sari, it's gorgeous, peacock blue and covered with gold embroidery. I mean *covered*.

EDITH Gosh.

CISSY She told me her name's Jayanti.

EDITH Jayanti…

CISSY And she was there at the procession for King George's coronation and that's where she wore the sari and these women from India marched with a suffragette banner.

EDITH I say.

CISSY They were in the Empire section with the Australians and Canadians and all that but the Indian ladies were the most beautiful.

EDITH I wish I'd seen them.

CISSY But we weren't allowed to go to the coronation parade. Papa won't let me go to London. Not even to Letchworth.

EDITH We're supposed to stay at home.

CISSY How am I ever going to get out and do anything if I just stay indoors and practise the piano like a mollycoddled miss? Jayanti is right.

EDITH Right…

CISSY	After all we're terribly privileged. It's not like we have to toil in the paddy fields all day.
EDITH	No.
CISSY	We have an easy life. It's too easy. What are we doing with it?
EDITH	Um…
CISSY	It's like Lady Constance says, how can we serve?
EDITH	She served. But now she's really poorly.
CISSY	What a shame Mrs Bannerjee can't meet Lady Constance! Lady Constance is so inspiring. And her father was Viceroy of India too and she lived in India so they would have a lot to talk about.
EDITH	I wish we could see the world.
CISSY	Jayanti showed me a magazine with photographs of the coronation procession. There were hundreds of Suffragettes there, all dressed in white. I don't care what Ma says – they looked glorious. And they were led by a lady on a white horse, in silver armour with a huge banner, like Joan of Arc leading her troops into battle, shining like a beacon because she was on a mission from God! Risking everything. Everything Edie!
EDITH	Everything.
CISSY	That's the life for us, isn't it? Not taking minutes and writing letters. We must do more. Deeds not words. Agreed?
EDITH	Deeds not words. Like Lady Constance.
CISSY	Agreed. Now I have a plan… Have you got any money?

Music – 'March of the Women'.

SCENE 8

1912. A house in London which has been turned into a suffragette HQ. HARRIET, a suffragette organiser, is busy. CISSY and EDITH enter, wearing coats and carrying a holdall each. CISSY's bag is over large.

They wait for HARRIET to pay attention to them. She finally does.

HARRIET   Yes?

CISSY   Is this the WSPU house?

HARRIET   You know it is or you wouldn't be here.

CISSY   We've come to join.

EDITH   To enlist.

HARRIET   Really? *(She gets on with what she was doing)*. We don't need any recruits. Go home.

They wait.

CISSY   We mean it. We've come to enlist in Mrs Pankhurst's suffrage army.

HARRIET   Go home.

EDITH   I'm Caroline Farmer's cousin. She sent us.

HARRIET   Names?

EDITH   Er... Emma... Shepherd and

CISSY   Charlotte Williams...

HARRIET   Your real names, Miss Farmer.

EDITH   Edith.

CISSY   Cecilia Walters.

HARRIET   Age?

EDITH   We're both 21.

HARRIET   Of course you are. Who knows you're here?

EDITH	Nobody. I mean, Caroline…
HARRIET	Caroline will telegram your parents and say you're safe.
CISSY	No need…
HARRIET	I haven't got time to waste dealing with angry parents. Let's have a look at you. You appear to be healthy girls. No fainting fits? No migraines?
CISSY	No.
HARRIET	Good. Well there's no room here but I can send you to our house in Bayswater. I hope you've brought sensible clothes. *(She sees Cissy's bag)*. You haven't come for a month at the seaside Miss Walters.
CISSY	Sorry. I couldn't find a smaller bag.
EDITH	Told you.
HARRIET	And what can you girls do? Apart from play the piano and hold French conversation?
EDITH	We're jolly practical.
CISSY	Edith's good at drawing.
HARRIET	Drawing.
EDITH	I could do, placards and things…
HARRIET	Hm. We do need extra hands at the moment. We've just had eight women released from Holloway.
CISSY	Were they… force fed?
HARRIET	Yes.
EDITH	They're terribly brave.
HARRIET	They did their duty. So, are you ready to do your duty?
CISSY	I should say so! Er, ma'am.

HARRIET: This is a volunteer army. If you don't want to work, go home. Discipline is paramount. Early to bed, early to rise. You're not here to enjoy the bright lights of London, go to the theatre and suchlike.

EDITH: No ma'am.

HARRIET: There is a campaign and we all have our part in it. You will be given the correct leaflets to hand out, calling for the clause to be added to the Franchise Bill.

EDITH: Is that it? Adding a clause.

HARRIET: Yes, that is it. One clause can give the vote to women. A simple message. Our aim is to make sure that message hits home.

CISSY: Forcefully?

HARRIET: Forcefully.

CISSY: Oh good!

HARRIET: Are you girls quick on your feet?

EDITH: We play a lot of tennis.

HARRIET: I'll send you to Bayswater this evening. You'll be under the command of Mrs Farebrother. You will follow her orders – this is a London wide campaign and co-ordination is vital. There are to be no independent actions, do you understand?

CISSY: Er, yes…

EDITH: Will we meet Mrs Pankhurst?

HARRIET: Of course not. Right. Coats off. There's work to be done here. You can have a cup of tea and a bun in the kitchen afterwards.

CISSY: What do you want us to do?

HARRIET	There's always a lot of work when we've had prisoners released. Some can go back to their families but our eight ladies are here for a few days.
CISSY	Shall we help nurse them?
HARRIET	Certainly not. That's a skilled job. No, I have an essential task for you.

She hauls out a large basket of dirty washing and shoves it at CISSY and EDITH. It stinks. The girls recoil.

HARRIET	The scullery's through there. There's a bar of carbolic soap on the side.
CISSY	Washing?
EDITH	So much…
HARRIET	Of course. What would your linen be like if you'd been in prison for ten days? No clean rags if your… You can imagine.

The girls stare at the basket, imagining all too well.

HARRIET	Well go on. Get scrubbing. Oh, and you'll need these.

She gives them a small hammer each.

EDITH	For the washing?
HARRIET	For the campaign girl. You'll get your orders where to start. Tomorrow.

SCENE 9

Oxford Street. CISSY and EDITH, dressed smartly and carrying bags, are staring into the window of a department store.

CISSY	They do have some nice shops in London.
EDITH	Debenham and Peabody. I had a coat from here once. That's a pretty dress.
CISSY	Which one?
EDITH	The green linen with embroidery round the neckline.
CISSY	Mm. Ready? Wait for the signal…
EDITH	Is it nearly eleven?
CISSY	On the first chime…

The clock strikes. They both produce their hammers and hit the window. There is a massive sound of breaking glass.

They stare in shock, paralysed for a moment, then run off. CISSY dashes back to scatter some leaflets, EDITH drags her off.

CISSY and EDITH go on the rampage in London. They break windows all over the place, with growing confidence. They dash around with glee, scattering leaflets.

CISSY	What does Mrs Pankhurst say?
EDITH	'The argument of the broken pane of glass is the most valuable argument in modern politics.'

They reach for their hammers.

EDITH	Cissy I can see a policeman!
CISSY	They seek us here, they seek us there.
EDITH	The bobbies seek us everywhere!
CISSY	Are we in heaven or are we in hell…
EDITH	He's looking at us. Let's go.

CISSY	We should do this window.
EDITH	Leave it Cissy, we'll get arrested…
CISSY	Let's get arrested then.
EDITH	No! My Mum will go mad!
CISSY	We've been smashing windows for months and we haven't got arrested. What's the point?
EDITH	Our orders are – stay unseen. Strike again.
CISSY	But if we don't get arrested how will people know what it's all for?
EDITH	There's leaflets.
CISSY	They go straight in the dustbin.

CISSY holds up her hammer.

EDITH	Put it away! There really is a policeman.
CISSY	I don't care. Let them come for me.
EDITH	What will your father say?

CISSY steps out and waves her hammer around.

CISSY	Over here!
EDITH	People are staring…
CISSY	Good.
EDITH	Suppose you go to prison?
CISSY	Of course I'll go to prison.
EDITH	But would you…
CISSY	Yes I'll go on hunger strike.
EDITH	No! Say you won't Cissy!

CISSY	I can take the consequences.
EDITH	It'd be horrible! You might die!
CISSY	Don't be silly. I shall earn my hunger striker's medal.
EDITH	That's not what…
CISSY	VOTES FOR WOMEN!

The POLICEMAN grabs her as she is about to strike the window. EDITH shrinks back.

POLICE	Oh no you don't Miss…
CISSY	VOTES FOR WOMEN!
POLICE	You lot have done enough damage.
CISSY	Let go of me!
POLICE	Calm down Miss…
CISSY	POLICE BRUTALITY!
POLICE	Come along then.
CISSY	Are you arresting me?
POLICE	Yes.
CISSY	Haven't you got handcuffs?
POLICE	You want handcuffs?
CISSY	Yes! VOTES FOR WOMEN! DEEDS NOT WORDS! VOTES FOR…
POLICE	Pipe down Miss for heaven's sake…

CISSY continues shouting as she is taken away. EDITH flees, unseen.

CISSY	VOTES FOR WOMEN… VOTES FOR WOMEN…!

SCENE 10

The Vicarage, April 1913. CISSY is sitting sewing, very dejected. EDITH enters, cheerful, carrying a tennis racket and bag.

CISSY	Not more tennis.
EDITH	Sorry.
CISSY	Isn't April a bit early in the year?
EDITH	It's such a nice day.
CISSY	I wouldn't know.
EDITH	Miss Puller and her sister have invited us to play at Youngsbury this afternoon.
CISSY	You spend all your time with my brother these days, not me.
EDITH	I mean I'd much rather you were my partner but Pip's not too bad. He's actually improved a lot. So until you're allowed out…
CISSY	I'm not.
EDITH	You must be terribly bored.
CISSY	I'm imagining being in Holloway, sewing shirts.
EDITH	Your parents are being very stern. Pip thinks it's a shame you've been gated for so long.
CISSY	I wish I were in Holloway.
EDITH	Don't say that.
CISSY	If I'd been sent to Holloway I'd be out by now! I'd have had six weeks, not six months. And at least the warders there wouldn't look at you with a pitying sigh and say, 'we're so disappointed in you darling'.
EDITH	Can't you ask your parents if… I mean, if you've been sorry for long enough.

CISSY	Papa won't listen. He says there's nothing to discuss.
EDITH	You were too young to go to prison Cissy.
CISSY	It's a jolly shame I say! What is the law there for?

GEORGINA enters.

GEORGINA	You two are not supposed to be alone together. I promised your mother Edith.
EDITH	I'm waiting for Philip, Mrs Walters.

GEORGINA picks up the post from the desk. Among it is her NUWSS magazine.

GEORGINA	How is your mother Edith?
EDITH	She's joined the Women's Tax Resistance League. She's refusing to pay the rates on the shop.
GEORGINA	Oh.
EDITH	No taxation without representation.
CISSY	Good for her.
GEORGINA	Cissy.
EDITH	She says she's fed up with having her hopes dashed and now we've got another electoral reform bill but there's no mention of women's suffrage she's had it up to the eye teeth.
GEORGINA	We're all very disappointed.

GEORGINA exits with letters. EDITH checks to see she's gone.

EDITH	I've got something for you…

She pulls out a magazine from her bag.

CISSY	The Suffragette!
EDITH	Caroline sent it.

They look through it excitedly.

EDITH	Look – Mrs Pankhurst's trial. They sentenced her to three years' penal servitude! It was a disgrace! They didn't even accuse her of doing anything, just inciting 'persons unknown' to blow up an empty building.
CISSY	She'll go on hunger strike.
EDITH	Of course. Then they'll let her out and arrest her again when she's stronger. Well, let them try! That's a photograph of some of the Suffragettes coming out of prison.
CISSY	They're so thin.
EDITH	They'll go to Mouse Castle.
CISSY	What?
EDITH	Mouse Castle. It's in Campden Hill Square in London. The Mice go there to get nursed better but the Cats know about it and wait outside. Caroline's been there. She says it's quite comical. These big policemen patrol up and down the street, all day and night. When someone comes out of the house, they compare her with the photographs they have of wanted women. Caroline was sent to do some shopping and she says she went right up to the bobbies and stared them in the face.
CISSY	Did they arrest her?
EDITH	No but they checked her basket for bombs. But of course they can wait on Campden Hill Square forever because the Mice sneak out at night through the back alley.
CISSY	It sounds such fun.
EDITH	An actress lady from the Actresses Franchise League came round to show everyone how to disguise themselves and change their voice. Maybe make themselves into a little old woman.
CISSY	I'd be good at that.

EDITH	Caroline says they want to set up Mouse Havens all over the country so Suffragettes on the run have somewhere safe to go. Our shop would be ideal – but Mum would never allow it.
CISSY	No.
EDITH	Then I thought – maybe we could find a tumbledown cottage or somewhere and turn it into a cosy den for Suffragettes. We could bring them provisions before they escaped to Scotland. It would be so exciting…!
CISSY	Yes!
EDITH	But you're not allowed out.

They are both downcast. CISSY is on the verge of tears.

EDITH	Don't fret Cissy. Your parents can't keep this up for ever.
CISSY	Everything's happening out there without me! Now I know how Constance Lytton felt when they released her from prison because she was a Lady…
EDITH	And because of her heart.
CISSY	But she didn't want to be released. She wanted to do her bit! I want to do my bit!
EDITH	It's all quite dangerous now though Cissy. Everyone's so desperately angry. There's bombs.
CISSY	Good.
EDITH	You couldn't plant a bomb Cissy.
CISSY	Try me.
EDITH	Don't be silly.
CISSY	I want to do something. Look at me – I'm young and strong and I sit here sewing.
EDITH	We had a go.

CISSY   It's not good enough.

GEORGINA enters brandishing her Suffragist magazine, 'Common Cause'. They hurriedly hide their magazine.

EDITH   I'm just going Mrs Walters.

GEORGINA   No no, listen. There's going to be a Pilgrimage.

CISSY   Oh.

GEORGINA   A Women's Pilgrimage.

EDITH   You mean like to Walsingham?

CISSY   Is this the Bishop's idea?

GEORGINA   No it's Millicent Fawcett's idea. She believes we must do something, in the face of the government's implacable refusal to help us.

CISSY   So she wants people to pray.

GEORGINA   No it's nothing to do with religion. Head Office are calling it a Pilgrimage but actually it's a march. A giant, national march. Women from all over England will walk to London and there will be a big rally in Hyde Park on the 26th of July.

EDITH   People have done all that before though, Mrs Walters.

GEORGINA   In London, yes. We keep trying to convince the government. But what about convincing the nation? In fact, what about convincing the government that the nation is with us, because I do think it is.

CISSY   I can't see how a walk is going to help.

GEORGINA   It will show every single town and village the marchers pass through that the women who want the vote are not these reckless arsonists or stuck-up ladies in white muslin, but ordinary women. People will see that Suffragists are peaceful and respectable, and not deranged monsters.

CISSY   Huh.

GEORGINA   I think it's a very good idea. Ambitious but safe.

EDITH   Won't marchers will be walking for days?

GEORGINA   Of course! A Pilgrimage is not supposed to be easy. Women will show they are prepared to put up with hardship to win their rights. And the government will get the message that there is mass national support for the vote and that it's not just a few extremists making a fuss. Anyway, July – that's less than three months away!

CISSY and EDITH stare at her.

GEORGINA   We have work to do!

CISSY   Like what?

GEORGINA   One of the arms of the march will come down from East Anglia via Cambridge. Down Ermine Street to London – they'll go right through the village!

EDITH   Ooh. Will we join the march Mrs Walters?

GEORGINA   Oh no, we'll be far too busy! *(reading magazine)*. There's a meeting of the national Pilgrimage Committee in two weeks. A Mrs Katherine Harley is in charge. We're to tell our local federation if we can offer free overnight accommodation, camping grounds, barns…

EDITH   Oh I see.

GEORGINA   Or if we know of suitable boarding houses, clean but very cheap. Can we offer food? Local committees to start fund raising as soon as possible… Right, Cissy - make a list.

CISSY   But I'm not allowed to do anything except sew.

GEORGINA   We'll need to know what time of day they'll be coming through so we can lay on the right refreshments. I wonder when we might know numbers? Accommodation – we have the two spare

	rooms here at the Vicarage and I'm sure the paddock can be used for camping… Fund raising. Perhaps a stall, at Whitsun… What do you think?
EDITH	Er…
GEORGINA	Oh this is exciting. It will be such fun to do our bit! Now then, we have letters to write… Cissy?

EDITH stares. CISSY is in despair.

End of ACT 1.

ACT 2

SCENE 1

July 1913. The Vicarage. There are a couple of banners propped up, piles of leaflets, trays of plates and cups, biscuit tins. CISSY and EDITH are painting signs, CISSY with rather bad grace. EDITH sings 'Danny Boy' as she paints.

CISSY	How do you spell 'Lavatories'?
EDITH	Lava – tories.
CISSY	It doesn't look right. 'The Vicarage – Lavatories'.

GEORGINA enters.

GEORGINA	Good. A couple more signs like that Cissy. And you'll have to make sure there's a good supply of soap in there, and paper of course.
CISSY	Who said I was on toilet duty?
GEORGINA	People will be very grateful to have proper facilities.
EDITH	Yeh they'll be fed up of going behind a hedge. Anyway, I'm on washing up.
GEORGINA	They're scheduled to leave Buntingford at 9am, the day after tomorrow. Buntingford will supply them with packed lunches. Midday public meeting at Puckeridge. By the time they get here they will be ready for tea. Apparently there's a cyclist who goes on ahead to tell the supporters to put the kettle on. *(The doorbell rings)* Oh…

JAYANTI enters.

JAYANTI	Mrs Walters. I hope you don't mind my calling uninvited…
CISSY	Jayanti!
JAYANTI	Well look at this!
GEORGINA	How lovely to see you.
JAYANTI	I don't want to intrude Mrs Walters…

GEORGINA	Not at all. I didn't know you were in the area.
JAYANTI	I have come up specially. I was determined to join the march as it approaches London. I thought of starting out from Cambridge but I haven't had the time so I shall pick it up tomorrow from, er…
GEORGINA	Royston.
JAYANTI	Yes. Royston to Buntingford. And then the next day we shall pass by here.
GEORGINA	Then you must stay the night with us, I insist. Mrs Bannerjee, this is Cissy's friend Edith Farmer, a loyal supporter of the Cause.

JAYANTI and EDITH shake hands.

EDITH	Do you like our banner?
JAYANTI	Yes I do! Are you two going to carry it?
CISSY	Um. We'll put it up at the refreshment stall on the high road and then we thought we'd give it to anyone who wanted to take it into London.
JAYANTI	Why not take it yourselves?
EDITH	We're not walking.
GEORGINA	We're doing teas.
CISSY	And toilets.
JAYANTI	You're not walking?
GEORGINA	Oh there's far too much to do as it is. There's the refreshments. Accommodation to organise in the area. Then I've been helping arrange the public meeting that's going to be held in the middle of Ware when the Pilgrims arrive there in the evening. So we really haven't got the time to walk ourselves.
JAYANTI	But you have to join the Pilgrimage! You mustn't miss out!

GEORGINA	We'll be doing our bit. They also serve who only stand and wait.
JAYANTI	But Mrs Walters, this is an historic occasion. There has never been anything like the Great Pilgrimage before and maybe there never will be again. The young people mustn't be denied the chance to take part.
GEORGINA	I don't think I can spare them…
JAYANTI	Not just them. You too. You must join in!
EDITH	Yes let's, Mrs Walters.
CISSY	Edie. It'll just be a bunch of stout women in tweed singing hiking songs.
GEORGINA	Not tweed.
JAYANTI	What?
GEORGINA	Mrs Harley has asked the marchers not to wear tweed. It will make them look frumpy.
CISSY	They are frumpy.
JAYANTI	Come along Mrs Walters.
GEORGINA	I really don't like marches.
JAYANTI	This is different. It will be a happy occasion.
CISSY	No-one will get arrested, that's for sure.
GEORGINA	Mm.
JAYANTI	And you won't be tramping the grimy streets of London. You will be out in the lovely Hertfordshire countryside.
GEORGINA	Mm.
JAYANTI	Come with me tomorrow to Royston. We'll all walk together.

EDITH	Let's go, Mrs Walters. It's once in a lifetime.
JAYANTI	You can be back home at the end of the day.
GEORGINA	Well. Alright. Yes.
CISSY	I won't go. I don't mind staying here and doing the teas.
JAYANTI	Don't be a martyr Cissy, you must walk with us too.
CISSY	Father says I'm not allowed out.
GEORGINA	Yes you are. For this.
JAYANTI	Cissy?
CISSY	If I must.

SCENE 2

On the road, early morning. JAYANTI and GEORGINA standing ready to go. CISSY and EDITH have their banner. They are shivering a bit. CISSY is pointedly ignoring her mother.

Another Pilgrim, ALICE, comes up to them.

ALICE	Good morning ladies. Chilly isn't it, for July? Don't worry. You'll warm up quickly when we get going. Is this your own handiwork? *(She admires the banner)*
EDITH	Yes.
ALICE	Very nice. Where are you lasses from?
EDITH	Um. Quite near here actually.
ALICE	Is this your first day then?
EDITH	Yes.
ALICE	Welcome Pilgrims.
EDITH	Thank you. Have you come far?
ALICE	I'm from Nottingham.

EDITH	You've walked all the way?
ALICE	Not quite, I'll be honest. I walked as far as Thrapston. Then I was feeling a bit tired and dirty and I had a terrible sore knee. The nice Suffragist lady who gave us bed and breakfast said I should rest for a day. Then I got a lift from another lady who drove her own motor car! She was going to Cambridge so I joined the Pilgrims there and here I am.
EDITH	You've done terrifically well.
ALICE	I've been missing the nippers but I'm determined to get to London.
EDITH	You've got children Mrs…?
ALICE	Mrs Malcolm. Yes, three rascals.
EDITH	Who's minding them?
ALICE	Me sister. We both wanted to come on this march and show the world it's not just London women as wants the vote. But she's got five children and I've got the three, so we agreed it'd be her that stayed home. And when I look at me blisters at the end of the day I tell myself I'm doing it for her too and at least I haven't got eight kids traipsing after me. Ooh we're off. Raise your banner high girls!

ALICE starts singing their walking anthem, 'Day of Hope and Day of Glory'. JAYANTI and GEORGINA join in uncertainly. CISSY and EDITH mumble and look embarrassed.

CISSY	Have we got to be jolly the entire way?
ALICE	Singing lifts your spirits. There's been days when we really needed it, in the rain and when it was just one hill after another.
EDITH	What did you do in the rain?
ALICE	Got wet.
EDITH	You do need good boots, don't you?

ALICE	Mine have stayed the course. But this left one rubs a little. Blisters are your worst enemy.
EDITH	I bet.
ALICE	Day three was torture. We got to Newark. When I took off my boots that evening – blisters the size of pigeon's eggs on both heels. I had to burst them and some of the regular hill walkers gave me methylated spirits to rub me feet with. Ugh. I was in agony. I thought, am I losing a week's pay for this?
CISSY	A week's pay?
ALICE	Well it'll be two weeks in the end. But my husband said, you do what you've got to do girl. We'll get by.
EDITH	Does your husband support the Cause too?
ALICE	I wouldn't say support. He's not against it. He just can't see what we're making such a fuss about.
EDITH	Where do you work Mrs Malcolm?
ALICE	I'm a sewing machinist. I probably sewed the lace on your best blouse.
EDITH	Oh. I can do machining. I manage a haberdashery shop with my mother and we also do repairs and alterations.
ALICE	Your own shop? And haberdashery. That's good. People will always need buttons.
EDITH	Yes. And their waistbands letting out.
ALICE	Me name's Alice by the way.
EDITH	I'm Edith. Everyone calls me Edie.
CISSY	Cissy. No-one calls me Cecilia.
ALICE	Pleased to meet you. And what do you do Cissy?
CISSY	Um… My parents want me to further my education.

ALICE Ooh. Yes you should.

CISSY They think I should be a teacher. But I'd rather be a missionary to Africa.

ALICE A missionary?

EDITH Her father's a vicar.

ALICE I wouldn't fancy Africa. All them lions and tigers.

CISSY The problem is I don't think it's right to force the Bible on people who are probably quite happy believing the things they already believe in.

ALICE I'm with you there. You can't make people think something. You can only explain to them why it's a good idea. That's why I don't hold with this violence. If we were just to terrorise the government into giving us the vote, that wouldn't be any good. We wouldn't have changed their minds, we'd have just got there by force.

EDITH Some people never change their minds though.

ALICE Of course. Some folk will always be stuck in the past. But once we get the vote, most of 'em will see that it's not such a bad thing. Then one day they'll be amazed there was ever a time when women couldn't vote.

CISSY One day.

ALICE It'll come.

EDITH You're an optimist.

ALICE People do change their minds. I've stood there in meetings and watched it happen.

EDITH I suppose so.

ALICE I tell you, we came through this part of Leicestershire. Very rural. And we reached this village and it was… the cottages were falling down.

	And they had to get their water from a well. You can't imagine.
EDITH	We can. There are places like that round here.
ALICE	But we're near London! Folk are rich.
EDITH	Not the agricultural labourers. They're not rich anywhere.
ALICE	People were standing around in the high road. I thought, ooh, the mood is hostile. Anyway it turned out the labourers were on strike. They weren't hostile, just hungry. We'd been supplied a really good picnic the day before so we were able to give the children some food. Then we held an impromptu meeting.
EDITH	In the street?
ALICE	On this Pilgrimage we've held meetings in all sorts of places. Anyway, we explained that the whole reason for women to get the vote is to improve life for people like them. Especially schooling for the children, and health. Most men don't care enough about these things, so therefore the government doesn't need to care either. But women care about them every day - so if we were voting the politicians would have to take notice. And I was watching people's faces and I could see some of them were going 'oh... I never thought of it like that before.'
CISSY	Does that change anything though?
ALICE	Yes. Yes it does.
EDITH	And at least you talked to them.
ALICE	Yes. No-one else does.
EDITH	You could be a missionary to rural villages Cissy.

CISSY shudders. They shift the banner uncomfortably.

| ALICE | Is that heavy? |

EDITH A bit.

CISSY No.

ALICE and EDITH carry the banner. CISSY joins GEORGINA and JAYANTI walking together, still distancing herself from her mother.

GEORGINA Would you like a cockle shell for your hat?

JAYANTI Thank you.

CISSY Edith made them. She's clever at things like that.

JAYANTI What is it?

GEORGINA It's an emblem for pilgrims. In the middle ages people who had made the pilgrimage to Santiago de Compostela in Spain would be given a cockle shell to prove they'd made the journey. It's a bit Catholic but there we are.

JAYANTI The distances people go for their faith.

CISSY Do you have pilgrimages in India?

JAYANTI Often. To the holy places.

GEORGINA London is our holy place this time.

CISSY The sacred site of … Hyde Park!

JAYANTI Shall we cleanse ourselves in the waters of the Serpentine?

GEORGINA Ugh! *(They laugh together)* Was your lecture tour successful?

JAYANTI The meetings were well attended. We raised funds.

GEORGINA Oh good. I'm sure people were terribly interested in what you had to say.

JAYANTI Perhaps. I was a novelty. I think they came more to see my sari than me.

GEORGINA	Oh surely they wanted to know about your work. Education is so important.
JAYANTI	Of course the Suffragists were very kind. But so often I was welcomed as a 'representative of the Empire'.
GEORGINA	People are devoted to the Empire Mrs Bannerjee.
JAYANTI	But I'm not representing anything, I'm just a person. They seemed keen for me to affirm that women of the Empire supported the suffrage cause.
GEORGINA	How marvellous.
JAYANTI	But… what about women of the Empire getting the vote?
GEORGINA	They have! In New Zealand and Australia. They're the pioneers! Oh. You mean in India.
JAYANTI	Mm.
GEORGINA	I'm sure you will one day. There's talk that India could have its own national parliament.
CISSY	You could even have self-rule.
JAYANTI	We could even have independence.
GEORGINA	But why would you want it? India gains so many benefits from being in the Empire!
CISSY	How do you know mother?
GEORGINA	I've been to talks by missionaries who are doing marvellous work out there. Mrs Fawcett is a strong believer in the Empire. She says it can be a huge force for good all around the globe. Without the Empire all our nations would be disjointed and alone.
JAYANTI	We know men believe that women cannot think for themselves…
CISSY	Typical nonsense!

JAYANTI   But I see now that the British believe Indian people cannot think for themselves.

GEORGINA   Well…

JAYANTI   People must have the right to control their destiny.

GEORGINA   The people of India will one day, when they're ready for it.

JAYANTI   Ready?

GEORGINA   I'm sure you'll agree Jayanti, not everyone is as educated and thoughtful as you.

JAYANTI   Educated – but for what?

GEORGINA   A nation has to earn its autonomy through making progress, just as women have earned the vote.

JAYANTI   India must prove that she's ready to govern herself?

GEORGINA   Yes or things will descend into chaos.

JAYANTI   But why should we have to prove it to the British?

GEORGINA   Because they're…

JAYANTI   In charge?

GEORGINA   Of course.

JAYANTI   But who put them in charge?

CISSY   They put themselves in charge. I mean 'we' did, I suppose.

GEORGINA   But look at what the British brought – order, and railways and… I mean you've benefited…

CISSY   You know very well the British ransacked the place Ma.

GEORGINA   Years ago yes. There was a lot of bloodshed. But things are different now…

JAYANTI   I don't deny I've benefited, myself. I just ask – how did the British put themselves in charge? In India, everywhere. How did the men put themselves in charge and keep themselves there?

CISSY   Wars.

JAYANTI   Force.

GEORGINA   Yes. Force. It's always force.

Pause. They walk on a little. A whistle blows.

ALICE   Lunch stop.

CISSY   Finally.

They get out their picnics.

GEORGINA   Let's share.

ALICE cuts up a large pork pie.

EDITH   That looks lovely.

ALICE   The lady in Thrapston made it.

GEORGINA   Suffragists are the best cooks.

EDITH   True. The food at Suffragette HQ was hopeless.

JAYANTI   No thank you. I don't eat meat.

ALICE   Oh. What do you eat then Mrs Bannerjee?

JAYANTI puts out a dish.

EDITH   That's nice. What is it?

JAYANTI   Pillau rice with vegetables and spices.

ALICE   May I try some? *(She tucks in, with pleasure)* Oh! That's delicious.

They eat happily, sharing the food. There is a sound of distant shouting.

ALICE   What's that?

She gets up, alarmed. GEORGINA gets up too.

ALICE   Can you hear it?

GEORGINA   I can hear people shouting.

ALICE   I hope…

GEORGINA   What?

ALICE   I hope there's not going to be any trouble.

GEORGINA   Why would there be trouble?

ALICE   There has been… in some places.

GEORGINA   What sort of trouble?

ALICE   In some places there were… crowds when we arrived. I mean they weren't very friendly.

GEORGINA   Why not? This is a peaceful march.

ALICE   I know but… Mansfield was the worst. It felt like there were thousands of people there, booing and jeering and mocking. It was terrible because Mrs Fawcett was with us that day. I don't know what she must have thought. People had to tell her it wasn't like that in every town…

GEORGINA   Like what?

ALICE   We had everything thrown at us – mud, rotten vegetables. Dead things.

GEORGINA   Ugh.

ALICE   Rats with maggots bursting out of them. And just… the names people called us… the words they used… We held a meeting and this mob kept rushing the platform and trying to throw the speakers down.

GEORGINA   Were there no police?

ALICE	There were but they didn't do anything. I said to one, look someone's going to get hurt. But he said oh it was just lads having a lark. Not my idea of a lark.
GEORGINA	It sounds horrible.
ALICE	Maybe someone had stirred them up. You know, the anti-Suffragists have been going ahead of us, holding a rally in a town just before we arrive.
GEORGINA	There are always opponents of the Cause.
ALICE	I don't understand why they had to be so nasty.

They hear shouting again. ALICE jumps and GEORGINA is nervous.

ALICE	Do you think…?
GEORGINA	I'm sure it's nothing.
ALICE	Some of the ladies said it's because folk think we're Suffragettes, come to burn down their houses.
GEORGINA	There have been dozens of arson attacks this summer.
ALICE	But there's been news in all the papers that this is a peaceful march. We've not broken a single window. There's no call to treat us with violence. I don't understand the reason.
GEORGINA	People don't need a reason to be nasty. They just need an excuse.
ALICE	Silly that it bothered me so much. But… there was nothing to warrant violence like that!
GEORGINA	How did you manage to carry on?
ALICE	What do you mean?
GEORGINA	Knowing that the next town might have another angry mob baying for you.
ALICE	Whenever we have an unfriendly meeting we hold another public meeting the following morning.

GEORGINA   In the same town?

ALICE   Yes. People are usually more sensible in the morning. We can get our message over and they listen. And we're showing them we're not afraid.

The others have been eating and laughing. The whistle blows again.

ALICE   Already?

They rejoin the others.

GEORGINA   You've eaten all the pork pie.

JAYANTI   How many people are here today do you think? It looks like nearly a hundred.

ALICE   It's been different day to day. One day the organisers told me there'd been 300 people on that stretch of the route. Then there's all the other routes coming in from other corners of the country.

GEORGINA   Some have come from Carlisle. They started weeks ago.

ALICE   Yes the ones who've come down the Great North Road.

GEORGINA   They're not far away. They stopped at Letchworth last night and today they'll be en route to Hitchin, Stevenage and Knebworth, spending the night at Welwyn.

ALICE   There's bound to be a lot more people joining as we get near London.

GEORGINA   Like us. Do you think we're cheating? Just coming in for the final few miles, the labourers in the vineyard at the twelfth hour?

ALICE   Cheating? It's not a competition.

They pack up their things, take their jackets off – it is hot now.

CISSY   Hard work though. How did you manage to walk day after day Alice?

ALICE	One foot in front of another.
JAYANTI	You must feel very proud to have come so far.
ALICE	I am.

GEORGINA takes up the banner as they move off, singing.

SCENE 3

Music – Auld Lang Syne

January 1914. The Vicarage. CISSY is sitting reading. EDITH enters.

EDITH	Happy new year.
CISSY	You too.
EDITH	The party was fun, wasn't it? Pip's a good dancer.
CISSY	Two left feet if you ask me.
EDITH	You danced with loads of people.
CISSY	It's my last chance before I'm walled up in the convent.
EDITH	You're only going to teacher training college.
CISSY	Same difference. I'll be a dull spinster all my life.
EDITH	Not you Cissy.
CISSY	I'll wear tweed.
EDITH	Why did you agree to go then?
CISSY	It's all I'm good for. I'm too stupid to do anything else.
EDITH	Don't talk rot. Just because you didn't get into Girton. It's terribly difficult to get into Girton.
CISSY	I knew I'd fail the exam.

EDITH	Run away to sea! Go and be a missionary! You wanted to go to Africa.
CISSY	I don't want to go to Africa any more – I'd rather go to Stepney.
EDITH	What?
CISSY	Sylvia Pankhurst is doing marvellous things there with her East London Suffragettes Federation.
EDITH	They say she's lost interest in the vote.
CISSY	Only because she's doing so much more. They've set up clinics and nurseries. They're helping the poor women by ensuring that their babies can live! That's the sort of thing that really matters, like Jayanti said. If only I were allowed to go and work there. I'd wash nappies!
EDITH	Can't you go? It sounds very Christian.
CISSY	Papa won't hear of it. He says it's a ridiculous fancy. It's alright for you. You've got the shop.
EDITH	Come and open a new shop with me. We'll open a supplies store for Suffragettes!
CISSY	Selling dynamite and chocolate!

They laugh. CISSY sighs.

EDITH	Can you believe it's 1914? Five months ago we were marching to Buntingford, remember? I felt so happy that day.
CISSY	We got our hopes up. We were fools.
EDITH	No…
CISSY	We felt so confident that we were in touching distance of the vote. The government promised Mrs Fawcett all sorts of things. And what have they done? Nothing.
EDITH	They might.

CISSY   They won't. They're mocking us. Sometimes I think the Pilgrimage was the worst day of my life.

EDITH   Getting arrested was the worst.

CISSY   No that was good.

EDITH   You nearly went to prison!

CISSY   But I wasn't scared because I knew I was doing the right thing. I felt free. Don't you remember running down Oxford Street with our hammers? No-one could touch us. I'd give anything to feel like that again.

EDITH   We were just girls then.

CISSY   And now we're going to be boring adults. With nothing to look forward to.

EDITH   You're completely wrong Cissy because there's the pageant.

CISSY   Oh not that.

EDITH   We've got to be in it! One thousand years of Hertford's history. That's not something you celebrate every day.

CISSY   There's only one thing worth celebrating and that's women getting their rights!

EDITH   But in the meantime there's the pageant.

CISSY   It's in the summer. Months away.

EDITH   They're already started planning. Everyone wants to take part.

CISSY   Not me. There's nothing in it for me.

Stirring pageant music.

SCENE 4

July 1914. First day of the Hertford Millenary Pageant. The grounds of Hertford Castle. A hot afternoon. JAYANTI comes on, carrying a knight's helmet and breastplate. She looks around uncertainly and goes off.

CISSY comes on, in ordinary clothes, carrying a bag. She looks around to see there is nobody else about and takes a can of paraffin out of the bag. She hears laughter and hastily puts the can back in the bag.

GEORGINA and JAYANTI enter, in high spirits. GEORGINA is wearing an ugly brown tunic, JAYANTI has the armour.

CISSY	You look like a sack of potatoes Mother.
GEORGINA	I'm a tenth century peasant.
CISSY	Couldn't they have given you a nicer dress?
GEORGINA	I like looking like a sack of potatoes!
CISSY	What are you Jayanti?
JAYANTI	Oh, I went into the costume room in the Castle and picked up what was left over. I haven't actually got a part in the pageant. I'm just background, you know.
GEORGINA	I'm in episode three – the Re-founding of Hertford by King Edward the Elder, 914 AD. Exactly one thousand years ago! Imagine!
JAYANTI	Of course we had flushing lavatories in India one thousand years ago.
CISSY	It's the most boring episode in the whole pageant Ma.
GEORGINA	Not at all. The first one, the Synod of Hartforde, is even more boring. In ours, the town of Hertford is arising from the ashes of war with the Danes. King Edward lays the stone and proclaims that on this spot a new borough shall arise. Then it's our chorus – 'Hartforde, thy star of fate, Dark clouds obscured of late Now, war's wild wrecking o'er, Shine forth for evermore…'

CISSY	Who wrote this codswallop?
GEORGINA	Mr Ashdown the Pageant Master. He churns out pretend Shakespeare by the yard.
CISSY	War isn't even 'o'er'. The next episode is full of it. Swords, arrows, the catapult thing.
JAYANTI	That's what everyone's looking forward to. The Siege of Hertford Castle twelve hundred and sixteen.
GEORGINA	As long as this trebuchet of theirs actually works. So far it hasn't managed to sling a bun. The Haileybury boys are getting very worked up over it.

JAYANTI holds up the armour.

JAYANTI	I could be a knight in the siege don't you think? With this helmet no-one would notice I'm a woman.
GEORGINA	You'd be just like Joan of Arc.
JAYANTI	It is not comfortable though.
GEORGINA	Philip says the chain mail is very scratchy.
JAYANTI	You try it Cissy. You haven't got a costume.
CISSY	No thanks.
JAYANTI	Why not? You should have a role.
CISSY	I'm playing my part.
GEORGINA	Go on darling. It's a once in a thousand year opportunity! Everyone is having such fun. 1914 will always be remembered for the Hertford Pageant!
CISSY	I'd rather 1914 was remembered as the year women got the vote.
GEORGINA	Oh Cissy. We keep pushing.

An announcer calls through a megaphone.

ANNCR	Episode three rehearsal. Members of the Moot, Thanes, Franklins, Hundredors, Masons and Citizens…
GEORGINA	Ooh, that's me!

She and JAYANTI exit, leaving the knight's costume with CISSY. She contemplates the helmet and breastplate.

EDITH enters. She looks stunning, in a beautiful dress.

CISSY	Gosh Edie.
EDITH	Do you like it? Mum and I spent hours on it. I think it's come undone at the back.

CISSY fastens her up.

CISSY	You're a princess.
EDITH	Oh no I'm just a maid in waiting. We don't say anything. We just gather round Queen Margaret of Anjou, in a sort of tableau. A herald presents the town charter and that's it. Nobody moves much except her horse. It poos everywhere.
CISSY	Did you really make the whole thing?
EDITH	We used every remnant in the shop. I'm jolly lucky to be in this episode. What are you?
CISSY	Nothing.
EDITH	Why have you got armour?
CISSY	I'm going to be Joan of Arc.
EDITH	She didn't come to Hertford.
CISSY	Pity. She would have livened the place up.
EDITH	But it's terribly lively! I had no idea so much had happened here.
CISSY	Oh Edie, it's just one thousand years of deeds of great men.

EDITH	That's what history is.
CISSY	Exactly. Apart from the odd Queen, who doesn't speak, a thousand years of Hertford's history is either men fighting or men droning on.
EDITH	Not altogether...
CISSY	Synod of Hertford – bishops droning on. Alfred fighting the Danes – women in the background wailing 'Woe! Woe!' Edward the Thingummy droning on, the French besieging the castle...
EDITH	But the Cadets are doing that so well...
CISSY	Suppression of Hertford Priory – Tudor men droning on.
EDITH	Visit of Queen Elizabeth to the town. Now that episode is fun.
CISSY	With more speeches by more men.
EDITH	And dancing.
CISSY	It's all men talking talking. Women standing around.
EDITH	You've got to admit it all looks pretty.
CISSY	Edie, doesn't it make you want to pick up a brick and throw it through a window?
EDITH	The Scouts wouldn't let you.
CISSY	What?
EDITH	The Boy Scouts are camping in the Castle grounds to guard against a Suffragette outrage.
CISSY	*(Putting on helmet)* We'd be in disguise.

They laugh.

CISSY	I just... when I saw the costume room in the Castle I couldn't help thinking what it would be like to put a match to the whole lot.

EDITH	Cissy!
CISSY	Burn down Hertford Castle and finish the job started by the French in 1216. It would be Joan of Arc's revenge. She'd show them.
EDITH	You do look like the cover of the Suffragette magazine. But she's not a good heroine to have Cissy – she got burned alive. And for what? Why do all the heroines have to be martyrs?
CISSY	No-one would get burned alive. There's no-one inside the castle right now.
EDITH	You can't destroy the costumes. People have put months of work into this pageant!
CISSY	I know I know. But you've got to admit the Suffragettes' arson attacks really have the government on the run.
EDITH	I don't like the arson attacks. They've gone too far.
CISSY	It's the government's fault. They've asked for it by completely ruling out women getting the vote. I say it's war now.
EDITH	Stop thinking about the vote Cissy for once. Enjoy the sunshine.
CISSY	Nothing's happening.
EDITH	It's all happening!
CISSY	I mean out there in England. I want to make something happen.

She reaches for her bag and almost shows EDITH what she has inside.

EDITH	The best things just happen by themselves Cissy. *(Pause)* Like Pip and me.
CISSY	Huh. *(She puts the bag down)*
EDITH	They've put him in charge of firing the trebuchet.

CISSY	Oh for heaven's sake.
EDITH	Don't you think he looks terribly handsome? Like one of the Knights of the Round Table.
CISSY	It's no good talking soppy about him to me Edie. He's my brother.
EDITH	He's asked me to marry him.
CISSY	Oh.
EDITH	What do you think?
CISSY	Well, good. Of course.
EDITH	I know he's at Cambridge and I sell buttons but your father has always liked me, hasn't he? He'll agree, won't he?
CISSY	Edie I'm sure he will.
EDITH	And you don't mind?
CISSY	We'll be like sisters.
EDITH	Exactly!
CISSY	I knew all along he was head over heels for you.
EDITH	Oh Cissy it's just so glorious. I can't tell you how glorious it is!

She laughs, gathers up her skirts and runs off.

CISSY, upset, goes and sits down, alone, out of sight.

GEORGINA and JAYANTI enter. They don't see her.

GEORGINA	Guess what? I've been roped in as a Frenchman.
JAYANTI	What do you have to do?
GEORGINA	No idea. Yell my head off and brandish my sword I suppose. Pip has finally got the trebuchet to work and then a scrap broke out with some lads from

Ware. Not Scouts I hope. They're expecting an attack, from Fenians I heard. They're all spoiling for a fight. It's been like that, this summer.

She totters slightly. JAYANTI catches her arm.

JAYANTI   Are you alright Georgina?

GEORGINA   It's hot work. I could murder a cup of tea but Mr Ashdown won't allow it. I… I don't think I'm cut out to be a Frenchman.

JAYANTI   Tell Mr Ashdown then.

GEORGINA   He doesn't like to be disobeyed. But the melée, people jostling me… and there was a feeling in the air… It reminds me… *(She is distressed).*

JAYANTI   What's wrong?

GEORGINA   It reminds me of Black Friday. Three years ago. You know the girls and I were there. Near the Houses of Parliament. We didn't mean to be. I should never have taken them… There was a huge press of people because the police were forcing everyone back and I lost sight of Cissy… I was trying to get through. This policeman stopped me. I said I'm trying to find my daughter and I thought he would help but he didn't he… he pushed me against the railings and he grabbed my… *(she indicates her breasts)* He just wrenched my coat open and… *(JAYANTI takes her hand)* It was really painful. And they were doing this deliberately. And, I'm a vicar's wife and everyone is respectful to me and policemen are respectful to me but there, in that place, I was just another woman and I was fair game. I've never told anyone.

JAYANTI   Not your husband?

GEORGINA   I wasn't sure he would believe me. I wouldn't blame him. Things like that don't happen to ladies like me. But you believe me?

JAYANTI   Yes. Did the girls know?

GEORGINA	No. I think now I should have told them, warned them what can happen, but I didn't want them to believe there is no order in this country. It seemed wrong to undermine their confidence in the police force.
JAYANTI	Suffragettes have brought complaints against the police you know. We can stand up to them.
GEORGINA	No. I don't to be a martyr, for the Cause or anything.
JAYANTI	No.

They sit together until GEORGINA feels calmer.

JAYANTI	We are going back to Calcutta in September.
GEORGINA	Ah.
JAYANTI	I'm ready to go.
GEORGINA	You have work to do there.
JAYANTI	Yes. I know now that we can't settle for a few crumbs of freedom from the Empire's table. I have learned a lot from the suffrage movement Georgina. I'm determined that we won't take the path of conflict and suffering to achieve equality for women.
GEORGINA	You might not have a choice.

Pause.

JAYANTI	Rest for a moment Georgina. Let me go and find us some water.

She exits. CISSY approaches. GEORGINA doesn't realise she has been there all along. CISSY looks at her disapprovingly.

CISSY	You didn't have to be a peasant Ma. Why can't you be Guinevere in green velvet?
GEORGINA	I know I look a crazed fool in a smock but Cissy, you have no idea how good it feels not to be the vicar's wife for once. I don't mind being a footsoldier.

CISSY | Well you should! All we ever do is serve in the infantry. Worrying that Father's alright, that Pip's alright, that we've written enough letters, raised enough funds so that other people can do things and get the glory.

GEORGINA | We're not in this for the glory.

CISSY | I know I know, service is its own reward and all that.

Pause.

CISSY | Why didn't you tell me?

GEORGINA | What?

CISSY | What you told Jayanti.

GEORGINA | Oh. That's all behind me now.

CISSY | You never told me.

GEORGINA | How could I darling? You were only 15. I had to protect you.

CISSY | What did father say? Did he notice?

GEORGINA | I told him I fell over. Of course, he was cross with me.

CISSY | How can you put up with it!

GEORGINA | You know how busy...

CISSY | I don't mean... I mean everything!

GEORGINA | It really doesn't bother me as much now. I mean, today brought it back... But most of the time I don't think about it. Alice changed things. Alice, on the Pilgrimage, remember? She said that every time they had a hostile crowd they put their fears behind them and held another meeting the morning after.

CISSY | But Ma how dare they! These men...how dare they... Why did nobody defend you?

GEORGINA   The thing is, there's not as much chivalry in the world as young people think. All these knights in armour, they're not really rescuing princesses.

CISSY   They don't even notice us.

GEORGINA   It doesn't matter.

CISSY   It does! What do we have to do to make them notice us! To see that we're persons!

GEORGINA   Do you know today I've been thinking about the Pilgrimage. Best day of my life.

CISSY   Admit it Ma, it achieved nothing.

GEORGINA   That's not true at all.

CISSY   A crowd of ladies had a jolly time. And nothing changed.

GEORGINA   Life is not like the history books. There are hardly ever any decisive victories. We make one step forward towards something better. Then another step. One foot in front of another. That's enough.

CISSY   How can it be enough? It's not enough. I don't understand how you can survive on so little!

GEORGINA   It's not little. I realised that on the march.

CISSY   The march! It wasn't anything. The rally in Hyde Park at the end – that was something. All those thousands of people with their banners, coming in from the four corners of London. That was glorious. But the march... really, it was just a walk.

GEORGINA   Exactly! We walked. And while we walked we weren't asking for anything, or being granted anything or denied anything. We hadn't chained ourselves to anything. We weren't arguing about things that shouldn't need arguing about. It was wonderful. For once I wasn't having to persuade or plead, or be clever or good. I only had to be me, a person, on a road. I was free.

CISSY   You see Ma. Deeds not words.

GEORGINA   Deeds and words.

CISSY   You do the words then.

Pause.

GEORGINA   It was a good day darling. Remember it. Once you know that you're free there's no going back. And this pageant. Of course it's all nonsense but join in. You're a child of a new century. Make this a glorious time to look back on.

A whistle blows.

GEORGINA   Sergeant Major Ashdown calls. Where's Jayanti? Vive la France! It's jolly being the enemy!

She exits. CISSY stands thinking.

CISSY   Deeds not words.

She puts on the helmet and the breastplate. She looks like Joan of Arc. She picks up her bag and takes out the paraffin can.

CISSY   They will take notice.

She takes out matches. Steels herself.

She takes a deep breath, tastes the air. Takes another breath.

Offstage, GEORGINA starts to sing their walking anthem from the Pilgrimage, 'Day of Hope and Day of Glory'.

CISSY listens to it, remembering, torn. She is shaking.

She puts the matches and the paraffin back in the bag. Fastens up the bag and puts it down.

She takes off the helmet and breastplate and lays them down.

She picks up the bag and runs off, as the singing dies away.

SCENE 5

Music – Keep the Home Fires Burning.

December 1918. A meeting of the National Women's Citizenship Society. GEORGINA is laying out a table with pamphlets, helped by a heavily pregnant EDITH.

EDITH	Who's chairing?
GEORGINA	Miss Puller.
EDITH	Just like old times. New name – National Women Citizens Association. Same people.
GEORGINA	The Cause is still the Cause. We keep pushing.
EDITH	I miss the cakes and sandwiches.
GEORGINA	At least we have tea, for once. I've been saving our rations. I've got some bacon for you.
EDITH	It's alright.
GEORGINA	I want you to eat well.
EDITH	There will be food, now the war's actually over. Won't there?
GEORGINA	Let's hope so.
EDITH	It's three o'clock. When are you going to vote Georgina?
GEORGINA	Later. There's so much to do.
EDITH	You should go. You're a 'person' now. Go and vote.
GEORGINA	It's so unfair that you can't.
EDITH	I know. Poor little baby. You'll have a mother who's not a person and no…
GEORGINA	The campaign goes on.
EDITH	Everyone's so tired though.

They busy themselves.

EDITH What is on the agenda today?

GEORGINA There's plenty to talk about. The hard work starts now, after all. All the things we said we wanted the vote for – better public health, housing, all that. Those are what we have to press for, now that we are finally full citizens. And by citizens I mean you too. How can the young women have worked so hard in this war, made so many sacrifices and not be deemed citizens? It's a disgrace! All those women who ruined their health in the munitions factories and still can't vote! I… well…

EDITH Calm down.

GEORGINA It makes me very angry.

EDITH They think the young and poor are all Bolsheviks.

GEORGINA Who could blame them if they were? Excluded like this.

EDITH Mrs Fawcett said we mustn't refuse half a loaf. Just keep demanding the other half.

GEORGINA At least once women are voting, the other half should come quickly enough. This time next year there will be full suffrage.

EDITH How many chairs should we put out? Do you think many will turn up?

GEORGINA I don't know.

EDITH Campaigning for public baths won't be as exciting as fighting for the vote. I don't think Cissy would be getting worked up over baths.

GEORGINA No.

EDITH I was thinking that before the war we had it easy. We knew what we wanted, we knew who the enemy was – poor Mr Asquith – and so we had no doubts about who we were. You remember when the war

	broke out the whole country was seeing enemies everywhere. And the worse the whole war has gone, the more frantically we've been creating enemies - conscientious objectors, people with a foreign sounding surname. Well, we haven't got the luxury of enemies now. We'll have to make our own way.
GEORGINA	You will make your own way Edie. And it will be a better way. I still can't stand Mr Asquith. 'The women have worked out their salvation in this war'. As if being a woman was some terrible sin that we have finally atoned for.
EDITH	This idea that they're graciously granting women the vote because we've earned it through our war work is just men's way of not backing down. Anyway, the women who worked the hardest haven't got the vote.
GEORGINA	We would have got the vote a lot sooner if the war hadn't intervened. I really believe that.
EDITH	If women could have voted in 1914, would we still have gone to war?
GEORGINA	Oh yes. Women were just as stupid as the men, everyone falling over themselves to embrace patriotic sacrifice. The nasty white feathers.
EDITH	I just remember everyone getting terribly excited. Pip insisting this was what they were preparing for.
GEORGINA	There was so much nonsense bandied about. War would bring out the best in the British character. War would purify the nation and make us strong again. Four years of national self-hurt. It didn't bring out the best in us.
EDITH	It did in a lot of women, surely? They've done things no-one thought they could do.
GEORGINA	Only because before they never got the chance.
EDITH	Yes, but you knew you could do things. Suffragists already knew what it was like to take action and make decisions. They organised a national

pilgrimage in four months. Other people didn't know what they could do until the war came. They changed.

A figure enters. It is CISSY, carrying a bag and wearing very battered boots and a dusty coat, under which is her VAD nurse's uniform.

CISSY   Hello Ma.

Her arrival is a complete surprise to GEORGINA and EDITH. GEORGINA can barely speak.

GEORGINA   Darling!

CISSY   Edie.

GEORGINA   I didn't know… why didn't you… when did you get back?

CISSY   The boat docked at five this morning.

EDITH   Why has it taken so long? We were worried.

CISSY   It's complete chaos in Belgium. They've got so many men to move and so many wounded. In the end I got fed up of waiting for some kind of transport and decided to walk to Dunkirk. It took me three days but I got there. *(She looks around)* What's going on?

EDITH   It's election day.

CISSY   Today?

EDITH   Yes.

GEORGINA   So later we're having a meeting to mark the occasion and discuss what we do next.

CISSY   And to have a party!

GEORGINA   Well…

CISSY   This is something to celebrate.

GEORGINA   Is it? Only half the job has been done.

CISSY   Still. What did it feel like Ma?

GEORGINA   What?

CISSY   To vote.

GEORGINA   Oh I haven't been yet.

CISSY   I thought you'd have been first through the door.

GEORGINA   We've been so busy. Oh Cissy. You're back at last.

CISSY   But just me. Edie, I've got to ask. Did Pip know? *(She indicates EDITH's bump)*

EDITH   Yes. He had my letter. It was returned to me with his effects.

GEORGINA   Let's get you home and fed and cleaned up.

CISSY   First things first. Let's get you to the polling booth Mother.

GEORGINA   I've time to go later.

CISSY   Go now. We'll come with you.

GEORGINA   There's chairs to put out.

EDITH   People can put out their own chairs.

GEORGINA sits down suddenly.

GEORGINA   I didn't think it would be like this. I thought it would feel glorious.

CISSY   Oh Ma.

GEORGINA   I used to dream of this day. I saw us marching to the polling booth in triumph. I never imagined that you two wouldn't be with me. I never thought I'd be tired and hungry and I'd have lost my son… It all seems so pointless now. Choosing between two dismal men. What difference will that make to anything? I don't want to vote.

EDITH	Don't say that!
GEORGINA	I don't want to vote when you two can't.
EDITH	But you must. You qualify.
GEORGINA	I don't want to qualify! I don't want the vote for being over 30 or a wife or a mother or for my sacrifices. I want it for being an adult human being. If I go and vote I'll be doing it on their terms.
CISSY	Pip would have told you to just get on with it.
EDITH	Yes.
GEORGINA	I don't want to vote when he's not coming back.
CISSY	I know.
GEORGINA	It doesn't feel like a victory.
CISSY	It's not. The victory was years ago. You told me that yourself Ma but I didn't understand. I wanted so desperately to win that I couldn't see that we'd already won. That day on the march when we were all walking and singing together, so many people with such very different lives but at that point we all knew that we were free, and equal to anyone. And all the government's obstinacy and violence was just spite because they knew women had won. This vote isn't a victory, it's a step. Come on. Let's go.

CISSY and EDITH help her up.

EDITH	We're coming with you anyway.
GEORGINA	I don't know what to do.
CISSY	Yes you do Ma. One foot in front of another…

They walk off together, as 'Day of Hope' plays.

THE END

Day of Hope and Day of Glory

by Charlotte Perkins Gilman

Day of hope and day of glory! After slavery and woe,
Comes the dawn of woman's freedom, and the light shall grow and grow
Until every man and woman equal liberty shall know,
    In Freedom marching on!
Woman's right is woman's duty! For our share in life we call!
Our will it is not weakened and our power it is not small.
We are half of every nation! We are mothers of them all!
    In Wisdom marching on!
Not for self but larger service has our cry for freedom grown,
There is crime, disease and warfare in a world of men alone,
In the name of love we're rising now to serve and save our own,
    As Peace comes marching on!

Verses adapted from the original and set to music for the play by Christina Raven

The March of the Women

Anthem of the Women's Social and Political Union (Suffragettes). Words by Cicely Hamilton, music by Ethel Smythe

Shout, shout up with your song!
Cry with the wind for the dawn is breaking.
March, march swing you along,
Wide blows our banner and hope is waking,
Sing with its story, dreams with their glory,
Lo! They call and glad is their word!
Forward! Hark how it swells
Thunder and freedom, the voice of the Lord!

Acknowledgements

Some sources for the plays:

- How, Anne, 'Jane Wenham of Walkern, England's last witch? 1712', in *Herts Past and Present*, 3rd edition, 1 (2003), 3-10.

- Swan, Annie S, *My Life: an autobiography* (London: Ivor Nicholson & Watson, 1934)

- Robinson, Jane, *Hearts and Minds. The Untold Story of The Great Pilgrimage and How Women Won the Vote* (London: Doubleday, 2018)

- Mukherjee, Sumita, *Indian Suffragettes* (Oxford: Oxford University Press, 2018)

- Marlow, Joyce ed., *Votes for Women* (London: Virago Press, 2001)

For more information on the plays and productions, see www.pinsandfeathersproductions.com

Cover design and artwork by Ken Boyter www.kenboyter.co.uk

Lightning Source UK Ltd.
Milton Keynes UK
UKHW020924301120
374346UK00009B/261